ALSO BY ANDREW HACKER

Money:
Who Has How Much and Why

Two Nations:
Black and White, Separate, Hostile, Unequal

Mismatch

---

*The Growing Gulf
Between Women and Men*

Andrew Hacker

SCRIBNER

NEW YORK   LONDON   TORONTO   SYDNEY   SINGAPORE

SCRIBNER
1230 Avenue of the Americas
New York, NY 10020

SCRIBNER and design are trademarks of Macmillan Library Reference USA, Inc.,
used under license by Simon & Schuster, the publisher of this work.

For information regarding special discounts for bulk purchases,
please contact Simon & Schuster Special Sales at 1-800-456-6798
or business@simonandschuster.com

DESIGNED BY ERICH HOBBING

Text set in Bembo

Manufactured in the United States of America

1   3   5   7   9   10   8   6   4   2

Some portions of this book are reprinted with permission
from *The New York Review of Books.* Copyright © 1979–2002 NYREV, Inc.

The statistics and test questions in chapter 5 are reprinted from "College Bound Seniors"
and "Sex Differences in Problem-Solving Strategies," with permission
from College Entrance Examination Board and Educational Testing Service.
Copyright © 1992 and 2000.

Library of Congress Cataloging-in-Publication Data

Hacker, Andrew.
Mismatch: the growing gulf between women and men/Andrew Hacker.
p. cm.
1. Sex role—United States. 2. Man-woman relationships—United States.
3. Sex differences (Psychology)—United States. I. Title.

HQ1075.5.U6 H33 2003
305.3'0973—dc21
2002030873

ISBN 0-684-86252-2

For Claudia

CONTENTS

Mismatch

PREFACE

*M*ismatch ventures into a terrain—the world where men and women meet—about which we all have opinions. This is hardly surprising. Almost everyone has lived near members of the other sex, starting with parents and siblings, continuing with classmates and colleagues, and on to spouses and lovers. Thus each of us has a wealth of experience and insights regarding relations between the sexes.

We could all write volumes on this subject. In fact, hundreds of authors have; many more if we count those who have penned novels and movies and television scripts. The book you have opened offers one writer's assessment of the state of the sexes in the United States today. My aim is to provide new information and interpretations that will help to shape and sharpen your own views. Most of the ideas ventured here will build on reliable sources, often from official documents and in statistical form.

However, there will also be times when hard evidence isn't available, or is in short supply. Then intuition and speculation must take over, and every effort will be made to present these interpretations as credibly as possible. This needn't mean that your agreement is expected on every page. Quite the contrary, *Mismatch* is a book to be argued with. And if you find yourself shaking your head, my hope is that you will also see enough here that makes sense so you will defer any doubts and continue turning the pages.

Mismatch has not been written as a textbook or an academic monograph. Rather, it is intended for an intelligent audience interested in a serious subject. For this reason, we begin with a caveat: some of the book's judgments may at first seem overstated, or appear to force the sexes into strict dichotomies. This has been done knowingly and for a reason. The ground where men and women meet can be a tense topography, where we are often on the defensive and ignore crucial truths about ourselves. One way to confront these realities is by portraying them as vividly as possible. In this spirit, hyperbole can serve a purpose: to sharpen our understanding of the murky world in which we live.

SEX AND STATISTICS

Most of the facts and figures that accompany the conversation in *Mismatch* come from government sources. The United States leads the world in quantifying the activities and attributes of its citizens. Almost all of these documents divide their tabulations by the sex of the persons. Yet these findings are dispersed in hundreds of documents the average taxpayer seldom sees. But they are public property, and it is our right to know what they say about us as individuals and about the country as a whole. In some cases, figures have been combined from several studies or categories have been compressed to highlight broader trends and developments.

It would be a mistake to view these tables as merely columns of numbers. The main reason we rely on statistics is that they provide precision. Figures can also tell very human stories and often surprise us with unexpected findings. For example:

- When the Bureau of the Census looked at wives aged 25 to 34 who had bachelor's degrees, it discovered that 35.6 percent of their husbands had a lower level of schooling.
- Figures from the Department of Health and Human Services show that 60.7 percent of divorces were initiated by wives, 32.5 percent were begun by husbands, and 6.8 percent were filed together.
- The National Center for Education Statistics tells us that among the graduates of dental schools, 40.1 percent are now women, compared with 0.9 percent in 1970. And women now receive 68.5 percent of veterinarians' degrees, up from 5.8 percent in 1970.

- The National Center for Health Statistics also has figures going back to 1970, which show that 72.9 percent of women college graduates began having children before they reached thirty. Now only 35.7 percent are giving birth that early.
- When the Internal Revenue Service looked at people who made more than $1 million a year, it found that 93.1 were men and 6.9 percent were women.
- The Federal Bureau of Investigation reported in 2001 that 7,783 men and 926 women were charged with murder or non-negligent manslaughter. For embezzlement, the numbers were 6,284 men and 6,293 women.

WHY *MISMATCH*?

Mismatch has been chosen as the title for this book because the term best characterizes how relations between women and men have been evolving over the last half century. In earlier times, the sexes were seen as complementary. Needless to say, nature and culture caused men and woman to differ in many ways. Still, it was assumed that their traits and temperaments formed a symmetry that allowed them to live closely and compatibly, with each bringing distinctive qualities to a common enterprise. Not only did nature intend for women and men to meet and mate; couples were so composed that they could reside contentedly for the rest of their lives. And by and large, they did.

Needless to say, not every pairing was a paragon of harmony. Battles between the sexes were doubtless common in every era, as memorialized in the bickerings of Shakespeare's Petruchio and Katherine, and Beatrice and Benedick. Yet by the final act, the shrews had been tamed and the bulls brought into an enclosure. In the aftermath, mutual obligations arose, to be fostered not only by the partners, but by the broader community, which had a stake in seeing matches succeed. The hope was that each partner would care for and about the other, providing the emotional comfort and support that most of us want and need. For an intimate pairing to succeed, each partner had to subsume a portion of the identity he or she brought to the match. If this was done freely, in return for love, so much the better. But in those days, the basic bond was founded on inner convictions of honor and duty.

If this symbiotic relationship was seen as natural, it was not wholly a reciprocal arrangement. As an ideal, complementarity supposes equal partners, with each one giving and receiving to the same degree. In reality, there was seldom such a balance, in marriages and less-lasting liaisons. The burden usually fell on the woman to make the pairing work. Thus when it came to consoling and commiserating, the man expected that the bulk of the attention would be bestowed on him. It was the woman's job to listen and understand; to sympathize when he suffered setbacks, to cheer his minor triumphs, and to show she was unequivocally on and at his side. If he asked about her day, his questions were usually perfunctory; nor was it always evident that he was absorbing her answers.

We know that women in earlier eras desired more equality and reciprocity at home and in the wider world. But few of them said so aloud, in part because there was little prospect that the other sex would alter its ways. Society offered few opportunities for women to fulfill themselves on their own, and in fact erected many barriers. So the woman contributed most to this arrangement, while the man received its benefits. To be sure, he had an excuse. He had man's work to do: protecting the household and providing its sustenance. He would arrive home pleading exhaustion. *"It's a jungle out there,"* he might groan, echoing his primal antecedents, as if to say that enduring this ordeal warranted his receiving the lion's share of attention. Though brief, this is not a wholly exaggerated depiction of the past. How far scenes like this have changed is a question that will recur throughout this book.

What *has* changed, though, is the readiness of women to subsume themselves or limit their ambitions to make life more congenial for men. Few are willing to sustain the former complementarity that required them to play a subordinate role. More broadly, they expect full equality, not just legally and in the economic arena, but in the holistic sense of being perceived as an integral human being. As hardly needs recounting, women are now entering spheres that were once dominated by men. And as more of them are revealing their talents, they are *competing* against men, a circumstance that was never contemplated in the past. Concurrently, today's high rate of divorce may be evidence of a growing estrangement, which transcends the difficulties of individual couples. Developments like these have begun to undermine what was once accepted as the affinity of the sexes. As a result, it is becoming increasingly difficult to describe today's women and men as a natural match.

Needless to say, the sexes are not always at odds; nor are all sexual tensions and frictions of recent origin. In some areas, men and women have similar ideas and attitudes. This will be seen in the chapter on children, where many couples are agreeing they want fewer of them. On another level, the power men have had over women has a long history, as will become apparent in discussions of why the double standard and physical assaults persist in our time. At the same time, these efforts at control—and women's responses to them—take on new forms and meanings in the current century.

Mismatch will also look at such phenomena as the growing number of fathers who are rejecting parental obligations, along with women who are choosing to embark on motherhood on their own. It will chart the changing faces of higher education and the workplace, as well as the repercussions of the growing acceptance of homosexuality. Other chapters will consider what "being a man" means today, and inquire whether the experience of black Americans has warnings for the white population.

As I suggested in opening this preface, all of us could write a book on men and women—or women and men, since the order makes a difference. It is also likely that each such work would reflect its author's experience and outlook, including the gender with which that person identifies. Does this mean it is impossible to be objective about how the sexes interact and regard and treat each other? After all, this arena is notable for rousing emotions and interests that color perceptions and interpretations.

This is perhaps a roundabout way of saying that I will leave it to the reader to decide how far what is said in this book rings true, or has enough plausibility to keep the conversation going. My early training was in political philosophy, at Amherst College and then at Oxford University, which focused on issues of freedom and justice and equality. One never forgets such studies, and their impress is on these pages.

Later, I did graduate work at Princeton and the University of Michigan, where my own field of political science was influenced by research in psychology and sociology. Since then, my teaching at Cornell University and Queens College has crossed academic boundaries, if only because the subjects I find interesting and important can't be encompassed by a single specialty.

This approach held for a book I wrote about the realities of race in America, where the inequalities faced by one race confront the insecurities of another. In a more recent book, on wealth and income, I found that people's goals were less purely economic than quests for status and esteem. Moving from race and wealth to the sexes seemed a natural progression, since it is another of this country's abiding divides. Here, as before, I use statistics when they can enhance our understanding, and add my own analysis when the discussion needs to be taken further.

An additional subtitle for *Mismatch* could have been "from affinity to estrangement." As women are becoming more assertive, and taking critical stances toward the men in their lives, they are finding that all too many men lack the qualities they desire in dates and mates. And despite bursts of progressive rhetoric, only rarely do men show themselves disposed to change in more than marginal ways. Thus there is a greater divide between the sexes than at any time in living memory. The result will be a greater separation of women and men, with tensions and recriminations afflicting beings once thought to be naturally companionable.

ANDREW HACKER
November 2002

1

Why Marriages Don't Last

Whether measured by quantity or quality, marriages are weaker and briefer than at any time since this nation began. As recently as 1970, among men and women aged 35 to 39, fully 83 in every 100 were husbands or wives. By 2000, the most recent Census count, the ratio had dipped to 64 per 100. On the other hand, the number of people who hadn't married, or no longer were, had doubled in a single generation. And among Americans who are currently wed, more now than ever are trying for a second or subsequent time.

There are reasons to be concerned. Marital failures have made us an unhappier nation than we would otherwise be, causing pain to young and old alike. Note, too, the amount of time and money and energy spent on dealing with the fallout from fraying marriages, with the range running from agencies trying to find defaulting fathers and outlays for child care, to toys purchased to assuage neglected children and cross-country visits to divorced parents.

Of course, marriage isn't the only possible bond between the sexes. Indeed, more Americans are spending more of their lives in a single state, and this seldom means they are staying celibate. The most common alternative is for two people to live together without a license, which increasingly includes having and raising children. At the same time, the great majority of women and men would like to see themselves married, even if not right away. They realize that doing so requires some kind of authorized ceremony, on a rather different plane from signing a lease or buying furnishings. Not only that, they want their wedded life to work and last, even if they are not wholly confident about that outcome. That said, the odds are that of every two unions now being undertaken, only one will be intact when one of the partners dies. This failure rate is both high and new. Yet despite the damage it causes, much of the debate about divorce is deceptive and evasive. Not the least reason is that the demise of lasting marriage asks us to look at facets of ourselves that we would rather not confront.

WHY OUR GRANDPARENTS
STAYED TOGETHER

One way to find out why so many marriages don't last is to consider why so many more did in the past. Every society has embraced some variant of marriage, and almost all prefer that pregnancies and births ensue after a wedding. A central purpose of marriage is to serve as a social constraint. Turning men into husbands and women into wives sets boundaries on their behavior. Thus a society will be more stable if, by nightfall, most adults are in their homes. Religions have also used marriage to control their communicants. Hence the traditional view that marriage is a lifelong obligation, inwardly accepted and outwardly reinforced, until a death brings a legitimate end.

And in the past, most unions endured. Wives and husbands grew accustomed to each other, largely by developing domestic routines. Romance, conversation, and mutually satisfying sex were seldom expected or experienced for long, if at all. For one thing, most households were large and crowded; for another, the work done by most men and women was manual and wearying.

At the same time, couples counted themselves contented, even if it was a quiescent affection. In large part, this was achieved because they were less married to each other than to the families they had created. To be sure, there were quarrels and sullen silences, and every community could cite cases of brutality and desertion. (The West was largely won by men who had run out on their wives.) Yet for all that, the conditions of marriages were not deemed to be a social problem. Most couples stayed together, and that was all that was asked.

Fast forward to today. As hardly needs saying, we can no longer assume that couples will stay together. Indeed, an air of resignation suffuses discussions of the subject. By any reckoning, too many matches deteriorate, often because they were misbegotten from the start. On the positive side, there are instances where breaking up has led one or both partners to find a fulfilling life they would not otherwise have known. (Although short of cases of molestation or assault, it is not clear that children benefit from having their parents part.) Even so, most people would prefer that every marriage succeed. Note how we harbor that hope for friends and relatives, even if we sense the odds aren't promising.

Why do people marry? At first glance, this may seem like a naive question; in fact, there's probably an answer already on your tongue. But when you think about it, you may find that there is no encompassing explanation, if only because there are so many intersecting reasons. Of course, most people will tell you they are passionately in love, with someone who is miles ahead of anyone they've ever known. From that ardor ensues a conviction they should spend the rest of their lives together, reinforced by a belief that their current compatibility will surely continue. Since that's how they feel, we usually nod and wish them well.

Simply stated, the decision to marry has two components, which are related but can still be considered separately. For the present, they can be characterized as the *why* and *who* phases in the process. The *why* behind a marriage begins when individuals conclude they would be happier married than in their current state. Even if they are active and busy, they still feel they are essentially alone, and believe their lives would come closer to being complete if they could share more of themselves with another person. Or they are or have been in serious relationships, but now want one that will have the imprimatur of a license. What is sought is intimate companionship, with someone who will provide support and sympathy and sex, along with the hope that your life will begin moving in new and more interesting directions. In at least a few cases, there may be a desire to become a parent, and most people still prefer to have this happen within a marriage.

But note: At no point thus far has anything been said about the particular person who will be the partner. That is the *who* component, but it is usually secondary to *why* considerations.

Once they begin moving through their thirties, most men and women begin finding fewer advantages in remaining single. It's not as if they actually tell themselves, *It's time I got married*. But even without so specific a declaration, something akin to it usually occurs, when people reach a point when they feel ready for marriage, and it should be the next step in the progression of their life. At such junctures, they find it easy to convince themselves that they've fallen in love with someone they've met, or perhaps have known for a long time. And since at any given time, a lot of other people are also tilting that way, it isn't hard to come across a kindred spirit with a similar inclination.

Along with the generic reasons, marriages often have more specific motivations, even if they aren't always realized by the individuals impelled by them. Here's a not uncommon sampling:

To show the girl who dumped you that you're not a loser.
Suddenly, it seemed all your friends were planning weddings.
Your mother hates her, so it's payback time.
You got pregnant, and things started speeding up.
She was older, so you would still have a mom.
He controlled your every move, and apparently that was something you wanted.
You fell for someone completely different, to waft you from a humdrum life.

Nor is it hard to think of other impulses that propel people into marriage, with each reason defining a circle of candidates. Thus in the instances just cited, specific searches will focus on people who are older or domineering or who make your mother crazy. On the other hand, to send a message to the lover who jilted you, or show your friends you can also find a partner, almost anyone will fill the bill.

As will be suggested later in this chapter, most of us are not strong on self-knowledge, nor are we all that adept at working out what makes other people tick. Over time, we are usually able to decipher the foibles of friends and colleagues; but these are more limited relationships, compared with committing to a lifetime with a spouse. Indeed, choosing a marriage partner is probably the worst possible occasion for making clear-eyed assessments. Once individuals become *marriage-ready*, they start looking not simply for a steady date, but for someone for whom they can feel an intense love.

In fact, this can happen quite quickly. The simplest reason is that those engaged in this quest are prone to project traits they find lovable onto the next person they find sufficiently congenial or pleasing. Scrutinize a woman and a man, both of whom are marriage-ready, where one is plighting a troth and the other is encouraging that overture. Even if they have been together for some time, they still know little about each other, because they are in a milieu where emotions eclipse reality. She has made him the lover she wants him to be, just as he finds in her qualities she doesn't really have, or they don't run nearly as deep as he thinks they do. In fairness, it should be said that she usually understands him somewhat better, since women have always augmented their power by sharpening their perceptions of men. However, this astuteness can be offset by her desire for a consuming love, which may blur her knowledge of what he's really like.

Even more anomalous, inherent in the choice of a partner is a prediction. If we observe a couple getting married today, each likes to think he or she has a grasp of what the other will be like, let's say, ten years later. But a lot of people change, often in unforeseen ways. In the past, this was less of a consideration, since people were expected to marry *for better or for worse.* Moreover, today's tempo has created more opportunities for women, leading them to rethink the kind of person they would like to be. Such epiphanies are less common among men, so a man may feel his union is going well, while she finds herself with a different view. Which shows there is no law stating that two spouses must grow and develop along mutually compatible paths.

WHAT HUSBANDS WANT

While generalizations are risky and exceptions can usually be cited, it is valid enough to say that men and women marry for different kinds of reasons. If this has always been true, that divergence created fewer tensions in the past, since mates settled for what they got. Now, being part of a pair is harder, as both seek more of and from a mate. In addition to the benefits that come with companionship, men also want something akin to a *nest,* to which they can repair and relax, with the domestic details in functioning order. Of course, modern men lend a hand, or say they do. In one Gallup poll, 73 percent of husbands said they pitched in with the cooking, which sounds good until we learn that only 40 percent of the wives said their mates showed up at the stove. (In a related survey, 89 percent of husbands said their homes had a fair division of chores, an assessmemt shared by only 55 percent of their wives.)

Along with being a *nest,* it is also a *lair* to which he returns after a day of hard and serious work. So even as men become husbands, they feel entitled to retain much of their freedom and independence. Given these priorities, they feel they can allocate only so much of themselves to a marriage, lest they impair the powers they will need to take on the world. (This also limits the time and energy they expend on the children.) And the same holds for attention to his betrothed. Of course, he loves her: truly, ardently, unreservedly. Yet in most marriages, he loves her less than she does him, largely because loving itself commands less of his life. Surveys also show that husbands express more contentment with their marriages than do wives. Even more telling, they are less apt to initiate divorces, and more than a few are surprised to find that their mates want to call it quits. Given what men want most from a marriage, most are satisfied with their version of a nest-cum-lair.

Needless to say, women want many of the same things. Yet they also tend to want more from a marriage: more than he does, or than he is prepared to contribute. Simply stated, women are willing to relinquish more for love, including changing their lives in substantial ways. And often they expect that through their marriage they will find new facets and dimensions of themselves. Indeed most look forward to this change, may have daydreamed about it, even exchanged scenarios with their friends. But few, if any, young men engage in these kinds of reveries. They may acknowledge that living with a mate will require adjusting their routines; but they don't expect they will have to alter their identity. With such disparate views of what should go into a marriage, brides and grooms are less embarking on a *journey* together, than on a trip with two separate itineraries and destinations.

Nor should anything said here be taken to mean she is insipid or imprudent. On the contrary, she may well have excelled in a demanding career. Rather, she has assessed the possibilities that the world offers and has decided what really matters to her. Indeed, it is not an exaggeration to suggest that today's women actually want more from life than men do. Unfortunately, when it comes to what women want from a marriage, not enough husbands are willing or able to provide the responses that wives believe are possible. As has been noted, this mismatch is not entirely new to our time. What is new is that women are now more likely to leave a marriage when they fail to get what they want.

It is a commonplace that girls mature earlier than boys, emotionally, intellectually, and in developing a sensitivity to the feelings and vagaries of others. Listen to the editor of *Maxim,* the magazine that has all but supplanted *Penthouse* and *Playboy.* "Now you have guys who are 35-year-old seventeen year olds." For American men, he added, "adolescence lasts until 35 or 40 now." This retardation cannot help but affect what they want in a wife. Just look back at high school and recall what boys sought in a date.

Of course, protests may be heard that much of what has been recounted here has an antediluvian ring. Hence it may be argued that attitudes have been changing, in particular that recent generations of men are showing themselves to be more responsive and mature in their relations with women. Certainly, ours is a more sophisticated age, and people know how to seem in touch with the times. (Thus hardly any husbands object when their wives opt to keep their own names.) The more crucial reality is that the shifts that are occurring are making it harder for members of the two sexes to adapt to one another.

SEARCHING FOR SEX

Now for a consideration that may seem tangential. Yet it conveys a lot about something that men want—and apparently aren't getting—from their marriages. Pornography is a national industry, and it caters as much to married men as to frustrated bachelors. Since there is so much of it around, there must be a market for it. In the past, patrons had to sneak into run-down cinemas, which were usually in seedier sections of larger cities. Now watching pornography is much easier and more widespread. Explicit sex is available for home viewing on DVDs and tapes, as well as on cable and hotel channels, and most prominently through the Internet. Men make up the overwhelming majority of the consumers. It isn't that women are puritanical, or turned off by close-ups of couplings, or averse to experimentation. Rather, they are more interested in knowing about the settings and surroundings of sexual acts, whereas men want to get right to the action.

What pornography does for married men is give them versions of the sex they would like to have at home, and most likely aren't getting, and may not even want to get. Primarily, they want to imagine themselves entangled with a partner who is with them solely for the sex and nothing else. Patronizing a prostitute is not enough to fulfill this fantasy. Not only would payment spoil the illusion, but most men cannot afford a quality of service akin to what they see on the screen. It is not that they regard their wives as virgins or saints. Rather, even in these liberated times, there are still things they feel uneasy asking them to do. For example, much of pornography is devoted to showing women arousing men orally, devoting more time and attention to these acts than tend to occur in marital sex. (Conversely, scenes of men doing the same for women are relatively rare.)

Also central to pornographic plots is that the women seemingly enjoy doing whatever the men want, all the while praising their potency and prowess. Whether or not this kind of fantasizing expresses a reversion to adolescence, it suggests that wives and husbands want different things from sex. The closest counterpart for women is the Harlequin-type romance. Even those that begin with the ripping of a bodice end up coupling sex with lasting love. And instead of depending on camera close-ups, the reader is free to formulate the pictures in her head. *

SEARCHING FOR MATES

Nowadays, finding a suitable mate requires a sustained search, since suitors on both sides set high standards and are more demanding. Ear-

---

*Women have also been making sexually explicit films. They are usually described as "erotica" rather than "pornography," and tend to be shown at art house festivals, often having lesbian themes.

lier, the decision was easier, since it involved less choice. Upon arriving at a certain age, it was something one did. Getting married and
starting a family was socially expected, and most people conformed.
Nor did one have to look far for a mate; your future spouse probably
lived nearby, and was someone you or your family already knew.
High school sweethearts would marry, often not long after graduation,
in many cases because the woman was pregnant. In 1960, the typical
bride was 20.3 years old, meaning that close to half of the women were
still in their teens, and her groom was under 23. Others met at college,
where the ritual of fraternity pinning was taken as a prelude to marriage. In a common scenario, the woman was a sophomore and the
man was a senior. So many coeds, as they were then called, cut short
their educations to become wives. If he went to medical or law
school, she would become a secretary to support him. (At his graduation, some universities awarded her a "PHT" certificate, standing for
Putting Husband Through.) And soon thereafter they started having children. In 1970, of the women having their first babies, 81.2 percent
were under 25; in 2000, births to mothers that young were down to
51.8 percent.

Clearly, things are very different today. Campuses no longer serve
as marriage marts, since young people now want a prolonged period
of freedom before tying a legal knot. They will say they don't feel *ready*
for marriage, which is essentially another way of saying that they
look forward to the excitement of independent living. They also feel
less pressured to marry because others think they should. By the
year 2000, the bride's median age had risen to 25.1, with 26.8 for the
groom, and most who were college graduates were waiting even
longer. Each year sees increasing numbers of first marriages with
both parties in their thirties. Unlike earlier times, when one's parents
or social group were involved in choosing a suitable mate, young people are essentially on their own. What they face is not so much a lack
of rules; by their mid-twenties, most are practiced in flirtation and dating. The problem, rather, is a paucity of settings in which to conduct
a search. Suburban shopping malls and corporate campuses offer
few opportunities for meeting and matching. City singles rely on bars
and summer shares, with perhaps a try at dating services, the Internet,
and personal advertisements. Television comedies must have this

audience in mind, since so many of their scripts focus on the difficulty of finding a decent date, let alone a long-term mate. Thoreau's phrase *"quiet desperation"* is probably too severe. Yet it is bemusing that a society that invests so much in offering such a vast array of pursuits and pleasures, falls so short in fostering what may be its most important relationship.

MULTIPLE MARRIAGES

Annually, some 2.3 million marriages are performed, and the total figure has remained much the same in recent years. What has changed is the status of the participants. In 1970, it was the first time for both in 68.8 percent of the ceremonies. By 1990, those who fell in this category represented only 53.7 percent of the total, and the figure is undoubtedly lower today. At last count, 8.7 percent of the brides and 8.5 percent of the grooms were affirming "I do"—or "I will"—for at least a third time. That so many keep on trying shows that the institution is far from moribund. Does this mean that Americans are incurable optimists, hoping against all odds that a Mr. or Ms. Right must be somewhere out there? The short answer seems to be yes. Even if the numbers are smaller, a large majority of men and women, including many same-sex couples, sooner or later want the imprimatur of a licensed marriage. At the same time, at least some of them must have thought that if it doesn't work out, they can always get divorced. So prenuptial contracts are no longer a rarity. While their stated purpose is to minimize discord if the pairing proves to be a mistake, their legal status implies they are meant less for *"if"* than *"when."* At best, they suggest a lack of certainty that this union will be a winner.

Nearly Everyone Marries was the cover message of a Census report issued early in 2002. And certain figures bear out that claim. When we look at people in their early sixties, 94.7 percent of the men and 95.2 percent of the women have been married at least once. If this is true, there doesn't seem to be much of a problem in finding someone to wed, since nineteen in every twenty people did.

But to point to people who are now in their sixties only tells us about members of an earlier generation. Today, 11.8 percent of women are entering their forties without having been married, as are 15.8 percent of the men. Both are the highest figures in this nation's history. The odds are also strong that most who remain unmarried this long are going to stay single. So what is now explained as a postponing of marriage may turn out to be a forgoing of it altogether.

WHY SOME MARRIAGES LAST

Of course, some marriages work. We all know of couples who have been married twenty or more years and still seem passionately in love with each other. Some look as if they have just come out of the bedroom, or can't wait to get there. We see them seated at a restaurant table for two, chattering together as if on a date, and not about the children. Or they may be sitting quietly at home, each engrossed in a book, but still very much together.

How do they do it? Every so often a Census statistician will hazard a personal comment, an intuitive insight based on years of parsing the figures. Here is one such observation, from one of the bureau's senior demographers, which he appended to a report on divorce:

> A certain amount of divorce undoubtedly grows out of the fact that those who would be most ideal partners never meet—or, if they do, do so at the wrong time.

Ideal partners. Of course! There is undoubtedly such a person out there, somewhere in the billions on this globe, who is absolutely perfect for you. (Indeed, there are probably several such people.) That person is so constituted that none of your habits will ever rub him or her the wrong way. You can go on being essentially yourself, and you will be loved just as you are. Moreover, you will feel the same way about your prospective mate. Sadly, the odds of these compatible spirits ever meeting are extremely low.

My own preference is to start with the premise that each one of us has a *temperament.* This term encapsulates the traits and tendencies that inhere in each of us, and which give us our distinctive identity. While we may characterize a person we know as, say, *"gregarious"* or, perhaps, *"moody,"* adjectives like these convey only part of who and what they are. Oddly, given our ingenuity, no one has devised a scheme for classifying human temperaments or creating terms to describe them. (The best we have done thus far is astrology, which assumes that our personalities were formed by conjunctions of the planets while we were in the womb. *"What's your sign?"* a man asks on meeting a potential mate, hoping to ascertain their compatibility.)

To advance this exercise, let's postulate that members of our species have twenty-four basic temperaments. There is no point in trying to give them specific names since, as was noted, each is a cluster of many attributes. Instead, we'll identify them by Greek letters. Let's say you are a *Theta*. (Where the letter is located in the alphabet has no significance.) What is important for our purposes is that certain temperaments are so constituted that they have a complementary relationship to some others. Thus your being a *Theta* accounts for the bond you have with your close *Kappa* friend. (Some temperaments may cluster in one sex, although there are androgynous exceptions.) At the same time, you may not get on as well as you might like with your *Delta* sibling. While she shares some of your upbringing and genes, this needn't mean that your temperaments will harmonize.

For an amiable mating, the challenge is to find someone who has a temperament that complements yours. Let's hypothesize that since you are a *Theta,* your best match for a marvelous marriage would be an *Epsilon.* With such a person, you would not only enjoy a lifelong idyll of love and friendship, but you could also be so suited that years would go by without a serious quarrel. (Other matches might join people who actually enjoy occasional spats.) How nice things would be if we all had our letters affixed to our foreheads, to reveal who we are and impart that information to an ideal mate.

Unfortunately, most of us have an imperfect understanding of ourselves, largely because we don't want to face up to the manner of person we are. As a result, you don't even realize that you are a *Theta*. Indeed, if you were told that this is what you are—and what it says about you—you would probably deny it with some vehemence. To continue this hypothetical example, let's say you think of yourself as an *Omega,* which you most definitely are not. So you have designed an

Omega mask, which you wear when in public, thus presenting an unreal image of yourself to others.

It is highly likely that sooner or later, you will meet an *Epsilon* who could turn out to be your perfect partner. Sadly, you are wearing that *Omega* mask, which just happens to set off all the wrong vibrations in someone who is an *Epsilon*. What makes matters worse is that the *Epsilon* you met is hidden under an *Alpha* mask, which you find somewhat repellent. Sorry, you have just met your ideal match, and you never knew it.

Does this sound familiar? Of course, it does, as it's the basic plot of dozens of movies. In the first scene, boy bumps into girl, and they take an intense dislike to each other. But the scenario being what it is, they are forced to work together on an important project. Or they get involved in an adventure, where they are pursued by a bunch of bad guys. As the story unfolds, both begin revealing qualities they never knew they had; and as that happens, they emerge from behind the masks they were wearing when they first met. By the end, they have become aware of their real selves and discover they've met the perfect mate. Surely, they'll live happily ever after.

Of course, this can also happen in real life. To be sure, there will still be occasions where negotiation and compromise are needed, as even the most equable among us will sometimes feel rubbed the wrong way. But getting things back on track is much easier when two temperaments have an elemental affinity.

As in the movies, some unions that turn out to be uncommonly successful begin for all the wrong reasons. The partners may have married knowing hardly anything about each other and made little effort to find out. Both may have been on a rebound, and wanted to show the person who dumped them that they were not losers. Or recall the man you said purposely picked a woman who would aggravate his mother. Yet in the course of living together, they gradually discover that they not only enjoy being with each other but that being together enhances both of their lives. How did they do it? The true answer is that they didn't do much at all. The chief reason is luck—the great good fortune of stumbling on an ideal partner, where both have winning numbers (or letters) in the lottery of love and marriage, where the odds are against most of the entrants. Indeed, a lot of people seem to sense this, as they cross their fingers when they make the marital promise.

WHY SO MANY MATCHES MISS

The designations *husband* and *wife* are not just words, but were meant as basic identities. Brides and grooms were expected to recast much of their attitudes and behavior, as they adapted to intimate living. To facilitate this process, men and women were assumed to be naturally matched, so what would start with sexual attraction could metamorphose into a companionable household.

As history and humanity evolve, so individuals alter the way they see themselves and what they hope for in their lives. Being a *husband* or a *wife* were identities devised in earlier eras, when opportunities were fewer and customs were ingrained. We are coming to realize that an apparent affinity was less a natural process than a cultural creation, built on an unequal distribution of status and power. Today, men and women have much more freedom, which often includes deciding how to delineate their lives. So while the terms *husband* and *wife* continue, they lack the authority and constraints they formerly had. In this environment, members of both sexes show less willingness to make the concessions and incur the obligations that a workable marriage requires.

2

Till Divorce Do Us Part

Each year, over a million marriages are dissolved, either by divorce or annulment. These finales are now so common that all of us know people whose marriages have come apart. At the same time, divorce isn't quite at the point where it is seen as *normal*, although in some circles it is now close to that. Most of us can recall being surprised when it happened to couples we thought we knew well. But there is also a foreboding that divorce is something many people will go through, possibly our own children or parents—or ourselves.

There are several ways to measure divorce, with each offering a different perspective on what is happening. The first is a *rate*, which calculates the number of divorces per year against the total population. During the last half century, the lowest rate was 2.1 per 1,000 in 1958, and it reached a high of 5.3 per 1,000 in 1981. In 2001, the rate was 4.0 per 1,000 people, which at first glance seems a marked decline from twenty years earlier. But this is a case where the statistics fail to tell the entire story, and the missing information will be provided later on in this chapter.

Another measure is a *ratio*, which compares the divorces in any given year with the number of marriages. That ratio is currently about 515 per 1,000 marriages. But this measure does not include data from California, Colorado, Indiana, Texas, and Louisiana, as they do not release their divorce figures. The ratio for Nevada is also omitted, since over half its marriages involve out-of-state couples who go there to be wed. So the 515 ratio is the total for 44 states, which are listed in the accompanying table. This is a notable increase over 1970, when there were 328 divorces for every 1,000 marriages, and almost

21

STATES OF DIVORCE
*Divorces per 1,000 Marriages**

U.S.A.   515

New Hampshire	959	Kansas	512
West Virginia	795	Kentucky	506
Oklahoma	772	Wisconsin	504
Washington	699	North Dakota	500
Arizona	681	Maine	486
Delaware	680	Connecticut	482
Mississippi	631	Illinois	479
Georgia	599	Minnesota	475
Wyoming	598	Virginia	467
New Mexico	597	Idaho	452
Missouri	589	Vermont	441
Michigan	589	Maryland	437
Oregon	585	Rhode Island	427
North Carolina	577	Tennessee	425
Florida	574	Massachusetts	421
Alaska	542	Utah	409
Ohio	537	Iowa	404
Montana	531	Arkansas	401
Alabama	527	New York	395
New Jersey	523	South Dakota	388
Nebraska	520	South Carolina	352
Pennsylvania	519	Hawaii	231

*California, Colorado, Indiana, Louisiana, and Texas do not release divorce figures, so a ratio with marriages cannot be computed. Nevada has not been listed because most of its marriages involve out-of-state residents. The U.S.A. ratio is for the 44 states in the table.

twice that for 1960, when the ratio was 258 per 1,000. Keep in mind that the marriages in the ratio all took place in the specified year, while those that are ending began at different times. Thus a daughter might be getting married just as her parents are divorcing.

Or we can simply look at the *percentage* of people who fall in the divorced category. Back in 1970, among women aged 40 to 44, only 5.6 percent were divorced and hadn't remarried. By 2000, the figure for the same group had grown to 15.0 percent. Divorced men in that age range rose from 3.8 percent to 13.2 percent. But those figures don't include all the men and women who have married again. The most current information we have comes from a 1996 Census survey, which found, that among men and women who have reached their forties, 32.3 percent had been married and divorced at least once. This is an appreciable increase over 1980, when the Census also asked this question, and only 18.2 percent said they had.

A final figure is a *forecast*: it tries to estimate how many current marriages, or those performed in a certain year, will eventually break up. Such statistics are bound to be speculative, since they are based on predicting how people will behave in the future. The most comprehensive study was released by the National Center for Health Statistics in 2001. Its forecast was that the first marriages of persons then aged 25 faced a 52.5 percent likelihood of ending in divorce.

WITH AND WITHOUT CHILDREN

While so much attention is paid to the fallout from divorce, it is important to distinguish those uncouplings where youngsters are involved from others that affect only the spouses. In fact, most concerns center on the impact on the children, emotionally and psychologically, and also financially, if their mother fails to get adequate support. Unfortunately, the most recent available figures are for 1990. In that year, slightly over half—53.0 percent—of dissolved marriages had children. The current figure has to be somewhat lower, as now there are more childless couples. So the good news is that fewer children are watching their parents get divorced. But there is another reason this is happening. Today, millions of youngsters aren't involved in divorces simply because their parents never married. As will be seen, they live in non-marital households, which have even shorter life spans than marriages, but whose breakups are not included in the divorce figures.

Since about half of the formal dissolutions involve only adults, it is appropriate to ask whether these types of divorces should be criticized. While one or both partners may experience personal pain, the great majority recuperate and go on to marry someone else. Nor are there signs that having had such a divorce hurts your prospects for another match; on the contrary, it may even make you seem more interesting. However, for another group of people who are divorcing, it's not as easy. Here the children are grown and gone, and (usually) the husband announces his intention to depart, whereas the wife would like the marriage to continue. In such cases, it cannot be said that both spouses come away unscathed. This kind of situation will be discussed later on in this chapter and in chapter 6 on the double standard.

As was noted, in 2001, the divorce *rate* was 4.0 per 1,000 persons in the population, which is visibly lower than the 1981 figure of 5.3 per 1,000. This decline is first of all due to the fact that fewer people are getting married, so there are fewer potential candidates for divorce. In the two decades from 1980 to 2000, while the population as a whole was growing by 28.4 percent, the number of married couples rose by only 14.7 percent. Even so, the divorce *ratio* continues to rise, because fewer new marriages are being matched by the ending of others that occurred in earlier years.

The most striking drop in weddings has been among younger couples; and they are the ones whose marriages are most prone to divorce. If we look back to 1970, in fully half of all divorces, the wife was in her twenties or even younger. In many of these cases, if not most, the partners simply weren't ready for so important a step. Also, at that time, about one bride in six was pregnant when she got married. Her condition usually precipitated the ceremony, which is not always the best way to begin a lifelong union. Today, it is much easier to end unwanted pregnancies—indeed, most are—so there are fewer rushed marriages. And if some women opt for abortion, others now feel freer about having and keeping a child without marrying the father.

LIVING WITHOUT A LICENSE

But what has really brought the rate down is that registered divorces are the only partings that are officially recorded. That is, the statistics are limited to relationships that were preceded by legal marriages. Today, almost half of Americans are reaching the age of 30 without having been married. As a result, there are fewer young wedded couples, who were once a prime source of divorce.

By the same token, what used to be first marriages are being replaced by periods when young people live together. True, some of these arrangements end in marriage; indeed, a wedding may have been planned beforehand. In a study of married women published in 1997 by the Department of Health and Human Services, 36.8 percent said they had lived with their husbands before marriage. Still, most *"cohabitations"*—the term sociologists use—don't continue very long. A 2000 study by Larry Bumpass and Hsien-Hen Lu of the University of Wisconsin found half lasted less than a year; and only one in six made it to three years; which left one in ten remaining as couples five years later. (Here the United States differs from European countries, where unmarried couples tend to stay together as long as their married counterparts.)

A generation or so ago, people made jokes about *shacking up,* a phrase that can still be found in most dictionaries. I prefer *"living together,"* which conveys what the arrangement is really about. A 2000 Census survey found some 3.8 million unmarried men and women sharing residences and usually a bed with one another, up from the 2.9 million in 1990. (Other studies put the figure closer to five million; it would go considerably higher if couples who maintain separate apartments are included.) For technical reasons, the Census gives one of the two the title of *householder,* even if both contribute equally to expenses. What was interesting is that the woman is listed as the householder in 44.5 percent of these homes, which usually means she is the owner or signs the rental lease, and the man is essentially her guest.

Of at least equal significance is the fact that 35.9 percent of the cohabiting homes have youngsters present. Some are biological offspring of the two adults; but most are only the mother's, and the man is her current boyfriend. So it would be premature to cast these arrangements as alternatives to marriage.

After all, most licensed unions last at least five years; and of those that break up, only a third do so that soon. There is reason to believe that as more people marry at older ages, or don't do so at all, many people will have several cohabiting relationships. Even now, 54.1 percent of all women who have reached the age of 30 have shared a home with a mate at least once, as have 45.4 percent of women who are now married, and 65.4 percent of those who used to be but no longer are. The last figure suggests that living together may be replacing remarriage to a greater degree than it is eclipsing first marriages.

The survey by the Department of Health and Human Services on cohabitation cited earlier asked women aged thirty through thirty-four about the outcomes of their first experience of living together. At the time they were interviewed, only 5.6 percent of the relationships were still intact; another 33.6 percent had broken up; and a much larger 60.8 percent had been followed by weddings. But it then emerged that three in five of those marriages had already ended in separation or divorce. One might think that living together beforehand would have made the couples aware of one another's foibles. Apparently not. Or if they knew what they were getting into, they decided later that it wasn't what they wanted. In fact, people who have *not* set up house earlier are more likely to have longer-lasting marriages. But this should be expected. For some adults, both premarital sex *and* divorce are moral offenses, and both are forbidden or frowned upon by their personal or religious beliefs.

Currently, almost 40 percent of children born outside of marriage, about a half-million babies per year, are to cohabiting parents. Mostly, the man in residence is the father, although not always, and about half of the mothers had earlier been married to someone else. So these relationships are not especially stable, even ones that ultimately end in marriage. The youngsters involved in them will spend less than half of their childhood with married parents; and when they do, one may be a stepparent.

WHY WIVES FILE FIRST

Probably the most popular depiction of divorce casts the husband as the departing partner. He tells her he wants out, saying he finds the marriage stifling, and sometimes adds he has found another woman who truly understands him and adds zest to his life. In this scenario, the couple has been together for at least a dozen years, and their children are at a difficult adolescent stage. In part, he wants his freedom as a recompense for lost, even wasted, time that he's spent focusing on a career instead of himself. He still sees himself as youthful and feels he is owed a second round. Nor does he believe he was a bad husband; he perceives the faults as largely hers. Why didn't she do more to keep herself attractive, and think of ways to have preserved his affections? For her part, she still loves him and wants the marriage to continue, even as he is insisting that it is over for him.

This is a familiar narrative. And the statistics do show that older wives in long-term unions are least likely to file for divorce. Having invested most of her life in making a home for her husband, she has learned to adapt to his habits and quirks. She may still love the guy, even knowing he is rejecting her and despite his infidelity. Given her age, she may feel that she has nothing to gain and much to lose by becoming single again.

Our concern here will be with the couples whose children are under the age of eighteen. These are the divorces that really matter, due to the trauma inflicted on youngsters and the economic outcomes for most mothers. So it may come as a surprise to learn that in marriages with children, the woman is the petitioner in 64.9 percent of the cases, which is considerably more than the 56.1 percent of divorces initiated by wives with no children in residence. Indeed, as the table on the next page shows, husbands make the first move much less than the wives in both kinds of divorces. The small percentages for joint petitions suggest that even with the "no-fault" option, amiable partings may be relatively rare.

The wife may be the one to take the first step for legal reasons. Even if the husband is the one who wants the divorce, in the end she may take the fault-based route, citing his infidelities or other transgressions

27

to obtain a larger settlement. While most mothers want custody of the children, they seldom have to fight for it, since few fathers want to become full-time parents. (Of course, he can pretend that he does, or propose an intricate dual arrangement, the better to beat down what he has to pay.) Still, these are incidental considerations. The bottom line is that in most cases, it is the wife and not the husband who wants to end the marriage.

Interviews of couples conducted since 1973 by the National Opinion Research Center consistently show that women are less happy with their marriages. Wives' feelings were also disclosed in a survey of

DIVORCE: WHO FILED?

Petitioner	All Divorces	Adults Only	With Children
Wives	60.7%	56.1%	64.9%
Mutual	6.8%	7.3%	6.3%
Husbands	32.5%	36.6%	28.8%
	100.0%	100.0%	100.0%

DIVORCE: WHO WANTED OUT?

Ex-Wives Said		Ex-Husbands Said
56.2%	I wanted the divorce or wanted it more	23.3%
21.5%	We wanted it equally	33.4%
22.3%	I didn't want it or wanted it less	43.3%
100.0%		100.0%

The men and women were from different marriages.

divorced men and women, conducted in the mid-1990s, which asked who most wanted the break. Its results are summarized in the table on the previous page. Of the former wives, 56.2 percent said they wanted out of the marriage, while 22.3 percent said it was their husband, and the remaining 21.5 percent reported it was mutual. With former husbands, it turns out that only 23.3 percent said they were the one who wanted the marriage to end, while 43.3 percent—almost twice as many—placed the onus on their wives, with the rest saying it was a joint decision. It is interesting and instructive that so many men were willing to tell interviewers that they wanted their marriage to continue, but their wives found them inadequate as mates.

ENDING ABUSIVE MARRIAGES

In all too many marriages, the husband continues addicted to drugs or alcohol, pursues serial infidelities, or torments the family with emotional bullying and physical assaults. In some instances, the wife's only recourse is to flee and find shelter wherever she can. Whether these cases are relatively rare or more common than realized is a recurrent subject for debate. And we are still trying to explain why as many women as do remain in relationships rife with cruelty and brutality. Even so, most victimized women eventually call it quits, often risking the wrath of husbands who continue to stalk them, combining protestations of love with their sadistic mode of showing it.

It is virtually impossible to find reliable material on this subject, since there is little agreement on what comprises abuse, and how to extrapolate actual cases from the smaller number that are reported. Throughout, an underlying issue is to what extent brutality is endemic to men. This question will be explored later on in chapter 8 on rape.

Official figures come from the Bureau of Justice Statistics, which estimates that some 900,000 women are physically assaulted each year by men who are or were intimately linked to their lives. About half of them file reports with a legal authority; and of those who do, half have injuries that require medical treatment. The studies also show that slightly over half of the assaults are inflicted by boyfriends, about 15 percent are by ex-husbands, leaving about a third by current husbands. (Much has recently been said about cases where wives do the assaulting. While such instances do exist, they usually reflect reports where the police ended up arresting both spouses.)

WHY PEOPLE DIVORCE

But physical violence, or drugs or alcohol, are not the usual reasons why marriages fall apart, even if fractious quarrels or sullen silences often signal that something is seriously amiss. A divorce occurs when one or both partners conclude that they cannot continue living with the individual who is their spouse. Granted, to say they *cannot* seems as if they're declaiming that they absolutely *must* leave, and if they don't, they will suffer serious harm. This is clearly the case when physical or emotional cruelty by one partner dominates the relationship. In fact, few people are frivolous about divorce. It is not just that they *want* to depart, but rather, they feel they truly have to.

In a classic study by Anthony Pietropinto and Jacqueline Simenauer, still as relevant today as it was when conducted twenty-five years ago, 3,880 men and women were asked to explain the rising rates of divorce. Their responses showed they had given serious thought to this question. Some of their answers, while succinctly stated, convey acute observations.

> People expect too much from marriage.
> Couples grow apart.
> People are selfish and self-centered.
> There is too much "I" in the relationship.
> People do not have a realistic expectation of what it is to share another's life.
> Women are generally the cause. They no longer treat their man like the head of the house.
> Couples do not communicate with each other.

Each one of these statements could have been expanded into a full book. In fact, there are shelves of such volumes, produced by therapists, academic experts, and authors recounting their own experiences.

Yet a lot of this material covers what we already know. By now, most Americans have either been through a divorce of their own or watched others at close range, augmented by the novels, films, and television shows that make it a central theme. Perhaps the most revealing observations are those that focus on traits of personality and character that can undermine a marriage. Of course, not everyone is *selfish and self-centered.* But a lot of people are, including many who are charming and attractive and fun to be with. What needs to be added is that today's society encourages, even approves, egoistic indulgence. Thus while departing fathers are not applauded, we hear little of the moral censure that was common in the past. And, as has been noted, most dads who defect have convinced themselves that the blame lies elsewhere and they had no other choice.

Needless to say, most women would not agree that *"women are generally the cause,"* and they would be right to roll their eyes on hearing this accusation. The problem, of course, is that there are still many men who want to be made to feel that they are the *"head of their house,"* and it is unlikely they will change this stance to any marked degree. In past generations, a wife who wished to preserve her marriage devised ways to lead her husband to believe he was the principal partner. Today, many women regard such behavior as demeaning and walk away from marriages that are based on subordination. So wouldn't it be equally accurate to reverse the statement, so it asserts that *"men are generally the cause of divorce,"* since so many have been unwilling to alter their outdated notions?

Or consider the statement, *"Couples do not communicate with each other."* This is a frequent complaint, again more common now than in the past. Granted, the term *communicate* is imprecise and has a range of meanings. It can occur in a tacit awareness of another's moods and needs, as happens in the best of marriages. Still, intimate relationships eventually call for conversations, of some frequency and duration. Or at least that is what growing numbers of wives want and expect. This demand is relatively recent: not too long ago, husbands who came home fatigued might groan about their day, but did not feel obliged to discuss what they did at work or on the way home. (Quips about wives calling the local bar must have reflected a fairly common occurrence.)

While modern men are somewhat more verbal than their fathers, not all husbands regard their wives as conversational companions. Her complaint, *"Why don't we talk more?"* is her way of saying she wants to exchange ideas and observations, as well as the details of the day. In this introspective era, there is an assumption that emotions and feelings will be discussed. Moreover, with increased numbers of women attending college, they are used to engaging in intellectual discourse, and have come to expect having such interchanges with their mates.

In a novel study, a dozen married couples, one or both of whom were graduate students, agreed to have voice-activated tape recorders run in their living rooms for a period of several weeks. Most of the time it was just the two people sitting together. What the tape took in over and over, were efforts by the wife to open a conversation, usually by asking her husband a question: about his work, his reaction to a news item, in fact anything. He would of course reply, but usually with only a word or two, and hardly ever showed an interest in following her cues. For her part, she would try to turn any remark he might make into a chance to get a conversation started.

While so small and informal a sample is not exactly science, its findings bolster the view that women are more likely to want the relationship to involve communication. More disturbing, the laconic responses by the men suggested that they did not consider their wives' comments to be worthy of thoughtful replies. This is in keeping with the way most of these men were raised: to believe that women were not their intellectual equals. Indeed, this leads to a basic question about coeducation. Observers of classes, from kindergarten through graduate school, note how seldom men and boys are attentive when girls and women speak. This has led supporters of colleges that enroll only women to question the presumed values of coeducation.

The individual who said that marriages founder because *"there is too much 'I' in the relationship"* got close to the core of the problem. For any marriage to succeed, it is just not enough to reach agreements about daily activities and long-term decisions. Something more crucial has to occur if a marriage is to thrive over successive decades. The *more* is that the two individuals must be willing to become quite different kinds of beings than the ones they had been previously. Not only must they begin to behave in new ways; they must also be willing to meld much of what had previously been their individuality into a collaborative life. (In theory, this would be easier for people who get married earlier, in that the two individuals could evolve together. In practice, as previously mentioned, such marriages have the highest failure rates.)

What is really required are qualitative changes in personal character, even identity. One needs to replace the notion of freedom with a subtler understanding of the self, such as when you no longer pursue some of your own interests, and discover—and enjoy—traits and talents you probably always possessed, but which only emerged by merging yourself with someone you love, admire, and respect.

Most women are less bound up with "I" than men, more willing to define themselves through a coupled life. Men think more about their independence and feel threatened by the prospect of merging, not to mention submerging, some part of themselves. By the time they marry, it is usually too late to break down this resistance. This seems to suggest that on the whole, women are prepared to put more into a marriage than are men. What is new is that all too many men are unwilling or unable to become the kinds of husbands modern women want. And that, in turn, goes a long way toward explaining why wives end up filing most of the petitions for divorce.

THE ARITHMETIC OF ADULTERY

Adultery apparently has a long history. After all, eschewing it wouldn't have been made a biblical commandment if it hadn't occurred with some frequency. Not surprisingly, there are no reliable facts or figures on its current incidence. The common problem with studies is that they ask people if they've strayed. While respondents are assured answers will be kept confidential, this is a fertile field for lying, even if it is to an interviewer they will never see again. As might be expected, most married men and women claim they have been fully faithful. Thus a nationwide survey, conducted in the early 1990s and sponsored by seven foundations, found 75.5 percent of husbands and 85.0 percent of wives asserting they had only engaged in sex with their spouse. Short of using hypnosis or lie detectors, which these researchers didn't do, readers had to judge for themselves whether these results seem plausible.

Here, as in other subjects, the allure is in the details: who did what with whom, where, and when. One such question is how far infidelities are the result of purchased sex. Considering the ubiquity of the industry, it is unlikely that all its patrons are bachelors. (Indeed, women who sell the services claim they have shored up many marriages.) At all events, surveys have been chary about asking for details on extramarital partners.

Cheating is often a cause or an accompaniment of divorce, even if it is not weighed in no-fault cases. In the study just cited, 24.5 percent of the men and 15.0 percent of the women admitted to infidelities, which might lead us to wonder *why* they were willing to say so. In fact, there is an answer. It turns out that over half of the men and two thirds of the women said their dalliances occurred during marriages that later dissolved. In some cases, these trysts may have contributed to the breakup or may have been symptomatic of other problems and not really a cause. In others, the marriage may have been effectively over, but the divorce paperwork hadn't yet been started or was just under way. In these interim periods, the soon-to-be-exes generally sleep separately, sometimes under the same roof but more usually apart. (In 2000, the Census found 7.2 million people who were still legally wed, but not living with their spouse.) If during this period they find someone new for solace, that also gets recorded as infidelity, but it is really only technically so.

Adultery takes many forms. It may be only one indiscretion, perhaps after an office party; or serial encounters, none of which really last; or a full-fledged affair that continues over months or years. All of these have been known to prompt the breakup of marriages that would otherwise have stayed intact, since there are spouses of both sexes who say they are no longer willing to remain with a partner after something like this has happened. There are also prominent exceptions, including the wives of several recent presidents, who chose to stay.

There are varied motives for adultery, ranging from pleasure, romance, and adventure to boredom, opportunity, and revenge. For men, the main reason hasn't changed since the commandment not to commit it was given. Many, probably most, men feel a need for repeated assurance that they are talented and attractive. Apparently they need more of this than their wives can provide, so they seek new sources of approval. An ability to charm other women into bed affirms that they are still the men they want themselves to be. Why so many men are so insecure in this area will be considered in chapter 7 on masculinity. Others just crave a conquest; here they're not looking to women for assurance, but rather to use and subdue them. These motives are akin to those that impel some men to rape, and will be analyzed in chapter 8 on that crime.

Married women are less inclined to stray. Things may not be going well at home; but they know that one or successive liaisons would be empty escapes. What such a woman wants is another chance at real romance, but finding it isn't easy on fleeting afternoons. Recall too that the women who had affairs were more likely than men to do so when their marriages were ending. Moreover, many women have active sex lives once they are single again. But this is no longer infidelity for them, although it may be for their partners, when they are married men.

Another issue is the logistics of adultery: where and when these trysts occur. For people who travel on business, this is not usually a problem. (Except for explaining why there was no answer when your spouse called your room.) But think about a suburban wife and husband, each married to someone else: dare they dally at local motels, when their SUVs are easily identified? Ingenuity is clearly needed. Or how does a mother of two arrange for an illicit weekend? Here is fallow ground for sociologists seeking tenure.

Still, statistics can tell part of the story, or at least suggest some leads. Adultery depends a lot on opportunities, which means available partners. For the sake of simplicity, let's simply look at married men between the ages of 40 and 44, when at least some start feeling their oats. And in an adjacent column, we'll put unmarried women aged 30 to 34, who might become possible partners. Back in 1970, there were 4.9 million husbands in the age range just cited, and 1.1 million single women ten years younger, which works out to 22 women for every 100 men. Today, using the same age groups, there are 3.6 million single women and 7.6 million married men, which now makes the ratio 47 women for each 100 men. So for this group of husbands, a potential pool for flings or liaisons has more than doubled, because there are now more women who haven't married or did but are divorced. Since they are in their thirties, almost all these women will be supporting themselves and have their own apartments. Most of them work alongside other women's husbands, which increases the imminence of intimacy. Of course, as we learned in Economics 101, a copious supply doesn't necessarily induce a demand. But it can—and often does—create temptations.

There is justification for our concern with adultery. Many if not most of us still consider it the acid test, not only of commitment to the marriage, but also of basic respect for your partner. Infidelity is a harsh assault where a spouse is most vulnerable. Too heavy a stress on jealousy can obscure a deeper issue. Knowing that the person you married has been unfaithful insults you personally and diminishes your worth. People can sexually fantasize as much as they like—it used to be called coveting. All of us daydream at a prodigious rate; indeed, most of society's erotica and pornography consists of pictures inside our heads. But fidelity means keeping your hands to yourself, not to mention other parts. Wives and husbands ask for this restraint, as an earnest of the esteem that eclipses all others. Even a so-called *"meaningless romp"* can scratch an indelible scar on a marriage, which is why those who stray take pains to conceal their assignations. (Unless, consciously or unconsciously, they want to get caught.) And in another reflection of how the sexes diverge, it is revealing that a man who has had successive flings feels he is entitled to become self-righteously irate when he finds that his wife has wandered once.

MAKING THEM STAY TOGETHER

If two adults decide to marry, no public officials or agencies have the power to deter them from obtaining a license and finding someone to officiate. When a couple decides to exchange vows, it is nobody's business but their own, assuming they are of different genders. If they choose to produce children, and afterward end the marriage, these are also freedoms that cannot be abridged. But as more parents divorce, the costs to society grow. By all measures, children from broken homes require more services than their classmates whose families stay intact. On the whole, these youngsters are burdened with more anguish during their childhood years, and that pain often remains throughout their adult lives.

If weddings can't be prevented, the incidence of divorce has stirred commentators to muse about measures that might keep more spouses together. Enter the American élan, which likes to feel we can solve any problem, if we put our minds to it. Thus lawmakers in Louisiana, Arkansas, and Arizona have created an alternative form of marriage, which they hope will become popular. Couples can opt for a "covenant marriage," which first calls for counseling to emphasize that they will be undertaking a lifelong commitment. While divorce would still be permitted, it could not use no-fault reasons like incompatibility or fading affections. Covenant partners would be expected to keep their pledge, with exceptions only for adultery, felony convictions, and "barbarous" abuse. During the first two years Louisiana had its law on the books, 3 percent of applying couples signed up for this type of marriage license.

Also in the 1990s, the Southern Baptist Convention, which governs a denomination with some 16 million members, resoundingly approved a resolution regarding marital conduct. It enjoined that a wife should *"submit herself graciously"* to her husband. For his part, he is obliged to *"provide for, protect, and lead his family."* The pronouncement, which women helped to draft, also decreed that *"the wife has a God-given responsibility to respect her husband and to serve as his helper in managing their household and nurturing the next generation."* It will be instructive to see to what degree this manifesto, and others like it, will influence the attitudes that women bring to marriage.

Directly or indirectly, marriage has entered the political arena. Here the rubrics *liberal* and *conservative* are not wholly outdated descriptions of positions and perceptions concerning family life. But it should be noted that it is incorrect to associate conservatives with a desire to maintain the status quo. After all, the current status quo contains legalized abortion, sex-laden soap operas, and bans on school prayers. Here and elsewhere, most conservatives want things changed. A better way to characterize their stance is to say that they wish to *restore* rules and regimens that prevailed in the past. Central to this outlook is the idea that a strong society requires a base of durable marriages; so conservatives tend to feel that divorces should be more difficult to obtain. However, their overarching goal is to induce spouses to stay together of their own volition. In their view, the current status quo often glamorizes divorce, and or at least presents it as an acceptable alternative.

Conservatives themselves know that they have an uphill fight. For one thing, commercial television and movies—part of the economic system they favor—have found that shaky marriages make for plots that raise sales and ratings. For another, a prominent fraction of their own leaders—Ronald Reagan, Newt Gingrich, Philip Gramm, Clarence Thomas, Strom Thurmond, Robert Dole—did not stay with their original wives. And Henry Hyde, who led the adultery-based impeachment of President Clinton, was found to have taken part in an extramarital affair, which led to the breakup of the woman's marriage.

Each year, however, another round of books appears extolling marriage and deploring divorce. Here some recent titles: *The Marriage Problem: How Our Culture Has Weakened Families; The Divorce Culture; The Broken Hearth: Reversing the Moral Collapse of the American Family; The Abolition of Marriage: How We Destroy Lasting Love.* By some lights, it may seem odd that conservatives are asking government to intervene in areas where choices have traditionally been left to individuals. Moreover, some of their proposals rely on idioms of psychology and counseling, a marked departure from the conservative doctrine of self-reliance. Of course, all political persuasions seek to use official power when it serves their interests and purposes. Businesses ask for subsidies while decrying stipends for single mothers, just as right-to-life advocates seek onerous regulations for abortion clinics. Little is gained by charges of inconsistency, let alone hints of hypocrisy. It may require some mental gymnastics, but we all feel we can show that, taken as a whole, our opinions are congruent and compatible.

The liberal posture is based on a quite different set of suppositions. The first is that individuals, especially women, should be able to pursue personal fulfillment. So if they feel miserable or stifled in a marriage, they may properly be encouraged to admit it was a mistake and move on. There is also the view that many marriages serve to suppress women; thus they are justified if, like Nora Helmer in *A Doll's House,* they decide it's time to quit. Insofar as marriage calls for give-and-take, for too long women have been doing most of the giving.

Because of the overlay of emotion and ideology, people usually look for studies that support their own convictions. So liberals tend to rely on research showing that women bounce back after divorce, that children adjust to life without fathers, and successive marriages can be a means to self-discovery. Stories are passed around of gatherings where stepchildren mingle easily with half-siblings and new companions of assorted orientations.

Liberals also like to be up-to-date and attuned to the latest trends. The idea of lifetime marriage can have an antediluvian ring, suggesting a partnership lived in a somnolent state rather than excitement and innovation. Nancy Dowd of the University of Florida titles her book *In Defense of Single-Parent Families,* where she claims that "research simply does not support the view that single parenting is harmful to children." Donna Franklin of the University of South California adds that society should learn to "accept the irreversibility of the high levels of nonmarriage." Still others ask for open minds about novel domestic arrangements. Schools are urged to have students in the early grades read books like *Daddy's Roommate* and *Heather Has Two Mommies,* whose titles summarize their stories. One aim is to instill tolerance toward alternative kinds of households. But another is to intimate to youngsters that they can choose such options for themselves when they are older. If conservatives build on religious tenets and moral principles, liberals emphasize social science research and psychological studies. Together, they select authorities that best substantiate their views. But wherever one sits on the political spectrum, the fact remains that a large proportion of the population will be touched by divorce. Perhaps those who will be affected most are our children, who are the subject of the next chapter.

3

Doing Without Dads

Fewer children now live with their biological married parents than at any time in the nation's history. The table on the next page shows that in 2000, those in other arrangements totaled 39.6 percent, well over twice the 16.6 percent of 30 years earlier. Most people are not pleased with this turn of events, as they feel that an original marriage is the best environment in which to raise children. Even so, the argument is increasingly heard that other arrangements can work just as well. Some add that there will be no return to earlier ways, so we had better learn to live with a redrawn domestic map. These changing configurations reflect the different choices made by adults. Today's men and women are exercising options few of them felt were available to them before, including the choice not to live with the person who is the other parent of your child.

Youngsters who aren't living with their fathers fall into two general groups. The first, whose parents are now separated or divorced, includes 52.7 percent of the children. For another 43.3 percent, the parents weren't married, and that figure represents a sharp increase from the past. (The rest live with grandparents or widowed mothers.) The reasons for the rise of divorce have already been considered, so this chapter will also look at the increase in out-of-wedlock births. A good place to begin is by examining how men and women are diverging in their attitudes toward parenthood.

AMERICA'S CHILDREN IN 2000:
WHO LIVES WITH WHOM

Married Biological Parents	60.4%
Unmarried Biological Parents	2.1%
Mother and Stepfather	5.2%
Father and Stepmother	1.4%
Adoptive Parents	1.0%
Foster Families and Others	0.8%
Mother Only	22.9%
Father Only	2.5%
Grandparents	1.8%
Other Relatives	1.0%
Non-Relatives	1.0%
	100.0%

Living with Half- or Step-Siblings*	13.3%
Living with Couples Who Are Not Married**	4.6%

*Includes with non-married parents.
**One adult may not be child's parent.

1970

Both Biological Parents	83.4%
Mother Only	10.1%
Father Only	1.8%
Other Households	4.7%
	100.0%

MEN'S LIBERATION

Until about the middle of the last century, men of all classes accepted fatherhood as a duty. This meant not only being a reliable provider but remaining with your family even when other options beckoned. The best evidence for that is that most of us can point to grandfathers who exemplified this model.

Each year, increasing numbers of men are unwilling to keep this commitment. As has been seen, less than two thirds of the nation's children are living with married biological fathers, and that figure only describes the situation to date. Altogether, as many as half of all children will at some time live in households without their father. Underlying this development are changing ideas about what being a parent does—and doesn't—entail. More adults of both sexes are embracing new freedoms and rejecting old constraints. In 2000, single women gave birth to 1,347,043 infants, the highest unwed figure in the nation's history. Needless to say, men helped to set this record, even though every drugstore now displays condoms, which can be easily purchased without embarrassment. So the rise in out-of-wedlock births suggest that one new freedom for men is to engage in unsheathed sex, which means either ceding birth control to their partner or risk beginning a pregnancy. (Nor do women always refuse if a man arrives unprepared.) Of the pregnancies that eventuate, about half are terminated. Most of the rest are producing a growing cohort of happenstantial children who are not only unplanned, but are the by-products of a new sexual latitude enjoyed by emancipated men. Men are spending less of their lives as resident fathers to children they have sired. And for their part, more women are deciding to become mothers and do the job on their own.

An astute economist named Stanley Lebergott coined the phrase *"men's liberation."* He was referring not to a sensitivity on the part of men to women's rights, but rather the freedom that enables husbands to leave their wives and children, with little or no social censure and seldom at drastic financial cost. As matters have turned out, it isn't so easy for others to be openly critical of such men. Most Americans now have friends or relatives or colleagues who have taken advantage of this emancipation. Elected officials and other public figures have also left their original families. Here, as elsewhere, a double standard persists. When a woman leaves her children, people shake their heads and wonder about her character. Moreover, much of the censure is internal: departing mothers seem less able to rationalize or rid themselves of guilt as fully as decamping fathers.

Of course, there are divorced fathers who obtain joint custody and are extensively involved in their children's lives. Others claim they want this, but are thwarted by their spiteful former wives. But the factual record is that fathers who live elsewhere are at best an ephemeral presence. After all, they aren't around regularly to help with school assignments, deal with problems in early stages, or get to know their children's friends. Rather, their being together usually consists of afternoon outings, meals at restaurants, and evenings watching videos, prompting tags like *Uncle Daddy* and *Treat Dads*.

In fact, these visitations tend to be sporadic. At best, for those living apart from their dads, only one child in six averages a weekly visit, while another one in four gets to see him about once a month. The most striking fact is that almost half have not been with their biological father for over a year. And a decade after their parents' breakup, two thirds have essentially lost contact with him. Whether due to chance or design or a bit of both, men often move to new localities after a divorce. According to one calculation, by the time the children have reached fifteen, their fathers are an average of 400 miles away. Irwin Garfinkel, a sociologist at Columbia University, found that four in ten divorced men who had children do not describe themselves as fathers. (As it happens, most of them remarry, which has consequences that will be described shortly.)

GOING IT ALONE

However it is viewed, this negligence on the part of so many men has led a lot of women to rethink the requisites of domestic life. Most still want to have and raise children, and increasingly they are prepared to do it on their own. Like many decisions, it also makes a statement, in this case that a viable family can be sustained without a male presence.

It further serves to highlight the shortage of reliable men. As was seen earlier, women initiate most divorces, even when there are children, and in many cases this means she will be raising them alone. But other women aren't bothering with the intermediate step of a marriage.

At one extreme are well-known figures like Jodie Foster and Madonna, Rosie O'Donnell and Wendy Wasserstein, along with Calista Flockhart of "Ally McBeal" and Camryn Manheim of "The Practice." Some have adopted children; in other cases, an obliging man provided what was needed. Single motherhood gained legitimacy in the 1982 movie *Tootsie,* where Jessica Lange played an actress who was raising her child without having been married. Ten years later, Candice Bergen's "Murphy Brown" made much the same choice, albeit softened by having her former husband be the baby's father. In the interim, Madonna's song "Papa Don't Preach!" dramatized a girl's determination to have and raise her baby.

Most single mothers who gain public attention have substantial incomes, so they can hire nannies and otherwise ease the burdens of parenthood. This can also be said of single women who adopt children, who now comprise about 30 percent of all adopting adults. Virtually all who choose this path to parenthood are at least in their thirties, enjoy middle-class earnings, and have shown they are ready to be parents.

As a result, we hear an explanation regarding why women are leaving marriages or aren't bothering with them. This one from *Newsweek* is fairly typical: "More women are better educated and better able to support themselves, so a husband is no longer a financial prerequisite to motherhood." While few people will contend that having a man in the house is an absolute necessity, some still feel that a good man can be pleasant and useful. For the present, though, we will look at how well mothers manage on their own. Pertinent figures, from the 2000 Census, are on the next page.

To start, only 13.2 percent of single mothers make more than $50,000 a year, which in many parts of the country would be an optimal income for raising children. But don't forget that out of these earnings must come expenses associated with working, not the least of which is child care. Further, more than four in five single mothers— the precise figure is 82.1 percent—have to cope on less than $35,000 a year, not an amount that leaves much for extras, let alone such essentials as snowsuits and sneakers for growing youngsters.

But doesn't the father have to pay child support? Yes, and some do. However, not all fathers accept responsibility for the lives they helped to create. Federal and state laws require that men remit something, and almost all counties have agencies that try to find defaulting fathers. These statutes also allow wages to be garnished, tax refunds be impounded, and DNA tests performed if paternity is denied. Some money is recouped, and may even get to the women who are raising the offspring of these men. But it can be a struggle. For example, some fathers are skillful at concealing income and assets. Or they suspend payments by claiming the mother has violated the terms of the visitation agreement. Moreover, most of the two million men now in prison are also fathers, but they are in no position to remit monthly checks. Altogether, only 16.5 percent of annual support awards are over $7,000, while 68.4 percent amount to less than $5,000.

The table on the next page, derived from a Census survey that appeared in 2002, shows that fully 41.5 percent of single mothers

SINGLE-PARENT HOUSEHOLDS: WHO MAKES HOW MUCH

Mother	Household Head	Father
4.7%	Over $75,000	12.3%
8.5%	$50,000–$75,000	16.4%
4.7%	$35,000–$50,000	18.4%
82.1%	Under $35,000	52.9%
100.0%		100.0%
$19,934	Median Income	$32,427

don't even have child support awarded to them. This happens most frequently when the woman isn't married to the father, and has no access to legal help or paternity testing. But only slightly more than half the divorced women get any kind of payment, and few of them have the resources to obtain compliance orders. In some bitter cases, women forgo payments because taking the money could give the fathers leverage about seeing the children.

Even among those who get something, the checks they receive *average* $3,844 per year, which means about half get even *less*. And remember that many of these households have several children. While the Census does not tell us the fathers' earnings, it offers a few clues. One is that mothers with bachelor's degrees averaged only $5,464 from the half of the fathers who paid anything at all. If most of these men are also college graduates with respectable incomes, it doesn't seem that the sums they are sending in will cause them much strain. So why

CHILD SUPPORT: AWARDS AND RECEIPTS

Twelve Million Custodial Mothers

Not Awarded Child Support	41.5%
Awarded but Not Received	14.8%
Awarded and Partly Received	16.8%
Awarded and Fully Received	26.9%
	100.0%

What They Got	Awarded Support	Received Something	Average Received
All Single Mothers	58.5%	43.7%	$3,844
Divorced Mothers	71.3%	55.1%	$4,611
Never Married Mothers	43.4%	29.3%	$2,676
College Graduates	68.9%	55.2%	$5,464

aren't fathers, especially those with professional earnings, made to pay several times the amounts currently awarded?

One way a husband gets back at a woman he once loved is by giving her as small a settlement as possible. That this could harm his children may not register with him, since what he sees is that the checks go to her. A further consideration is that most judges are still men. Consciously or not, they may put themselves in the shoes of parting husbands who will now have to maintain a separate apartment, continue payments on a car, and want to enjoy a few rounds of golf and occasional meals out. Typically, the living standards of divorced fathers in fact rise by 10 percent after the split, which is yet another benefit of men's liberation, while those of the mothers and the children fall by 27 percent.*

As has been noted, more former husbands than wives remarry, and this can affect the man's feeling of obligation toward his children. For example, his new younger wife may bring children of her own, and he finds he has to help with their expenses. Indeed, he may take this in stride, since he loves their mother, and no longer has such feelings for his former spouse. Or the new wife may be younger and hasn't yet had a child. He may be willing to remedy that condition: what better way to attest to his virility and renewed youth? But once this new brood gains priority, it leaves less cash for the offspring with whom he no longer lives, and whose mother may not speak of him in the kindest of terms.

No precise figures are collected on how many remarried men are starting second families. However, we have statistics that suggest the number is growing. When a child is born, the age of the father is entered on the birth certificate. Among men aged 40 to 44, a prime period for remarriage, those who are becoming fathers have been rising: their numbers are now 23.8 percent higher than they were twenty years ago. Indeed, older men, including quite a few in their fifties, are fathering more children. Some now have two sets of youngsters, separated by twenty or more years. That this is much rarer

---

* Each year, some fathers are arrested and charged with failing to send support payments. Federal attorneys secured 143 convictions in 2001, and 98 in the first half of 2002. These numbers should be set against the 7.6 million men who paid nothing.

among women may be taken as another expression of differential liberation, albeit possibly of nature's making.

In all this, it is hardly surprising that second wives have sided with their husbands. Some accuse first wives of living in luxury, while men caught in the middle strive to build a new life. In California, they have formed a group called COPS (Coalition of Parent Support) to press their case. In Indiana, former husbands have POPS (Parents Opposed to Punitive Support) to beat back bills aiming to raise payments and strengthen their enforcement.

MOTHERHOOD WITHOUT MARRIAGE

Among women currently raising children on their own, four in ten are described by the Census as *"never married."* Compared with divorced mothers, they tend to be younger, come from poorer homes, and have less education. Their incomes average $12,221, half of the $24,515 for women who had once been married. Of course, this isn't surprising, since we are comparing women who haven't been brides with those who were in marriages for several years or even longer. But what they have in common is that their children are being raised without a resident father. And they also share the situation of having made a child with a man who has either rejected that responsibility or whom the mother doesn't want in the home.

In 2001, exactly one of three American infants—33.4 percent—were born to girls and women who were not married. In 1960, by comparison, the ratio was one in twenty. During the decade that followed, the one identified with the sexual revolution, these births had doubled to one in ten, and they continued to rise, as the table on the next page shows.

The age when unmarried births occurs has also been changing. In 1970, half of these children were born to teenagers, which elicited considerable concern. But by 2000, girls and women under twenty accounted for only 28.0 percent of the total. So more babies are being born to older unmarried women; since 1970, the percentage has doubled among those over thirty. This shift suggests that fewer unwed births are due to youthful lapses, and more are conscious decisions, and often involve a second or later child. It is also important to note that by 2000, stringent rules concerning welfare were well under way; so it is not as if these choices were spurred by the idea that mothers could depend on public stipends.

In the early 1970s, half of premarital pregnancies led to marriage, whereas by the 1990s, less than a quarter did. By the 1990s, also, less than half—47.2 percent—of first children were conceived *after* marriage. Another reason why the non-marital ratio is higher is simply statistical: there now are fewer births within marriage. Couples who used to have three now stop at two, while others are having one or none.

There's a long-standing idea that single mothers are completely on their own, and that the child's father is either wholly out of the picture or an infrequent presence. While this is often the case, another kind of arrangement is becoming increasingly common. Currently, almost 40 percent of non-marital births are to couples who were already living together and thus bring the baby to a preexisting home. This is now happening across the social and economic spectrums, from those who reside in trailer parks to celebrity couples whose babies are heralded in fan magazines.

Another common belief is that unwed mothers carry something of a taint, and are unlikely to find marriage partners. A study by the

PERCENTAGE OF ALL BIRTHS TO UNMARRIED WOMEN	
1950	4.0%
1960	5.3%
1970	10.7%
1980	18.4%
1990	28.0%
2001	33.4%

Russell Sage Foundation tested this view by comparing these women with the majority who don't have children before marriage. Among those who avoided premarital motherhood, 88.3 percent had found a husband by the time they reached 40. And of those who started childbearing on their own, a respectable 71.7 percent were also married by 40, generally to someone other than the child's father. So it seems that men tend to spare judgments on this score, which should be welcome news. But the same study also found that "the presence of non-marital children increases the risk that a marriage will dissolve." In fact, this also happens when divorced women bring their children to a second marriage. Even if the new husband makes an extra effort, it is not always so easy to create amiable relations with another man's offspring, and thus the marriage may founder.

STOPPING AN AVALANCHE?

The numbers cited in this book have disturbed many people. Half of all marriages will end in divorce; close to 40 percent of children aren't living with their fathers; and now a third of all birth certificates don't have the woman's husband listed as the father. In all, the concerns are both moral and economic, accompanied by anxieties about the stability of society. To address the matter of births, in 1996, the U.S. Congress created a competition among the states, offering annual rewards of up to $20 million to those that showed the greatest reductions in their out-of-wedlock rates. (A proviso was added that the declines could not be due to abortions.) In 2000, Arizona was one of four winners, due to its rate dropping by three-tenths of a percentage point, from 38.5 percent to 38.2 percent. Measured in actual numbers, Michigan was also up there, since it recorded 719 fewer non-marital births, which by my calculation netted it $27,816 for each non-born child.

In fact, most liberals are not pleased with the out-of-wedlock statistics. While the publications of Planned Parenthood do not condemn unmarried mothers, they would prefer that there be fewer of them, largely because all too many of their children will grow up in uncertain surroundings. As is well known, they encourage the use of contraceptives, including by teenagers, and easier access to terminating pregnancies. This is common in other countries, where unmarried people are just as sexually active as in the United States. But as the table on this page shows, young women here are much more apt to become pregnant, and then are more likely to have the baby. Needless to say, their sexual partners also have responsiblity for these conceptions. Historically, there is a recklessness and bravado endemic to many American men, which is reflected in owning and using guns and courting risks while driving a car, and believing that having to stop and roll on a condom is something that a real man shouldn't be obliged to do.

For their part, conservatives object to any reliance on birth control and abortion, even if that would reduce out-of-wedlock births. Their preference is to recommend abstinence prior to marriage. Federal money already supports this approach to sex education, with the funding available to religious as well as public schools. There are no reliable findings thus far on what, if any, impact this curriculum has had. But it is a fact that teenagers are having fewer babies. Between 1991 and 2000, the rate fell from 62.1 per 1,000 to 48.5 per 1,000, a drop of 22 percent. Proponents of abstinence attribute this to their teachings. Others say the downward trend was under way even before the programs started, and reflects choices of girls who realize how they would be handicapped by early motherhood.

SEX, SWEDES, AND THE U.S.

Rates per 1,000 Girls and Women

	Pregnancies	Births
Sweden	25.0	7.8
France	20.2	10.0
Canada	45.7	24.5
Great Britain	46.7	28.3
United States	83.6	48.5

A 2002 proposal by the Bush Administration would spend $50 million a year to encourage young people to marry, and pay for counseling sessions designed to impart the "skills and knowledge" needed to keep their unions intact. Its proponents believe such urging is needed because, relative to the adult population, the number of marriages is at an all-time low. Another purpose of this drive is to reduce the percentage of out-of-wedlock births. Here too it will be instructive to see if this effort succeeds.

UNMARRIED FATHERS

While so much attention has been given to unmarried mothers, it's important to note that the fathers have managed to elude the spotlight. Now, as in the past, a double standard is alive and well. Since earliest times, fathers of out-of-wedlock children have not been censured or shunned. Some are even admired for their audacity. Grover Cleveland became president of the United States, Jesse Jackson remains a prominent spokesman, and John Forbes Nash, renowned as the subject of *A Beautiful Mind,* received the Nobel Prize. Prominent athletes and entertainers are regularly sued for child support, and leaving a trail of children often gains them more notoriety than reproach. It's almost as if their pursuit of conquests is taken as a given for their gender.

In the law designed to end welfare programs, passed during the Clinton Administration and with its encouragement, almost all its provisions dealt with making single mothers work. The message seemed to be that having an out-of-wedlock child was an unlawful act, for which the mother had to be punished. Even divorced women who had their children while they were married were, in effect, being chastised for not having kept their husbands. (By way of contrast, married women are often urged to stay at home, and are cheered for doing so.) But apart from attempts to get defaulting fathers to send support checks, no one has proposed stronger measures to deter irresponsible procreation. Imprisonment seems overly onerous; and to really be effective, it would have to be for life. (The actor Tony Randall fathered two children while in his late seventies.) Some men convicted of molestation have been ordered to be sterilized, but all those rulings have been overturned. And thus far no judges have proposed it for promiscuous fathering. Moreover, unlike mothers, the men who created the children were not consigned to compulsory work. And were this tried, they would undoubtedly claim it was involuntary servitude, which is expressly banned by the Thirteenth Amendment to the Constitution.

Every so often, an especially egregious case puts the issue in perspective. In 2001, a defendant came before Wisconsin's supreme court for being $25,000 behind in support for nine children he had fathered by four different women. A lower court had decided that if he sired a tenth, it would be deemed a violation of parole and he would be sent to prison. One justice argued against this ruling, on the grounds that "men and women in America are free to have children, as many as they desire," and "may do so without the means to support the children." While this freedom is nowhere specified in a law, our system presumes we are at liberty to do anything we wish, unless some statute specifically prohibits it.

And the likelihood is small that legislatures at any level will proscribe procreation. This may end up being one of those areas where most people don't favor government intervention, but still find themselves hoping that certain kinds of behavior won't occur. Like fathering nine children and walking away.

WHAT DO DADS DO?

Is a resident father necessary? Most people will agree that his presence can be helpful, and usually is. Let's start with the economic aspect. Obviously, a higher *percentage* of youngsters who live only with their mothers will be poor. In 2000, the Census found that 39.7 percent of them were, compared with 6.9 percent of children living with both parents. However, the actual *numbers* paint a slightly less skewed picture. Among those with incomes below the poverty line, 6.1 million are supported by their mother, compared with 4.2 million who have married parents. So for poor children, the ratio is that two have both parents with them, and three are residing with only one.

The median income of families with married parents ($60,168) is three times that for those headed by single mothers ($19,934).* Part of the gap is due to the fact that in most marriages, both partners are earners. But even when only the husband works, he brings in on average twice as much ($45,315) as a single woman will. So having a man in the house means that the children will benefit from the advantages that accrue from his income.

Some single mothers are independently wealthy or are in well-paid occupations, so they don't need a second income and can hire nannies for the children and other chores. True, it's not quite the same to send such a person to your daughter's soccer match or to take your son to the pediatrician.† Fathers can pitch in with such obligations; and if many don't help as much as they might, they are generally around when seriously needed. But is it only *fathers* who can do these things? That is, must a second parental figure be a man? Leo Tolstoy was raised by two aunts. And recall the children's book *Heather Has Two Mommies,* which has two caring parents, but not of different sexes.

Still, there is reason to believe that the two sexes tend to bring different aptitudes and outlooks to the rearing process, so both together can provide a more stimulating atmosphere. And a father may offer another approach to the guidance and discipline that most children need. This is especially the case with boys. As will be seen in a later chapter, fewer boys who were raised solely by mothers go on to college, compared with their sisters or with boys from two-parent homes. This said, we should be wary of sexual stereotypes. Two gay or lesbian parents can be as congenial a couple as a heterosexual pair.

Most adults who had fathers living with them when they were growing up will say they were pleased this was the case. But this needn't mean they got a lot of attention. In 2001, a team of social sci-

---

*Of course, the couples have the expenses of their second adult. As it happens, the two household types average about the same number of children: 1.97 for married couples, and 2.13 who live only with their mothers.

†In Florida, a divorced mother with a demanding law practice lost primary custody of her two daughters to their unemployed father. He declared that "dads can be moms, too," and his case was argued by a team of women lawyers, some of whom were also mothers. The former husband of Marcia Clark, O. J. Simpson's prosecutor, also sued for their children's custody, citing her long hours at the trial.

entists at the University of Michigan decided to clock how much time fathers spend with their children. The average was 63 minutes per weekday, of which 33 minutes were spent at family meals or watching television. On the two weekend days, the average rose to 166 minutes, with 54 for meals and television; but during much of the rest of the time, the mother was also present, as with family trips to church or the mall. Even when both parents are employed, mothers spend twice as much time reading to the children and helping with homework. Figures like these have led Frank Furstenberg, a sociologist at the University of Pennsylvania, to remark, "Once you have one good parent in place, having another parent in place doesn't have a huge effect on children." And Paul Amato of the University of Nebraska has wondered if "the extra attention of fathers may be largely redundant, once one takes into account the mother's involvement."

THE DAMAGE OF DIVORCE

As was noted earlier, traditionalists want a father in every home, regardless of the time he spends there, because they feel that is the natural setting for children. Thus they urge parents to stay together even if their pairing has palled. In their eyes, the motive of many divorces is to make life pleasanter for one or both of the adults, not to benefit the children.

With questions of this sort, preconceptions often intrude. Thus Francine Russo, writing in the *Atlantic Monthly,* invokes the justification that "children are less damaged by divorce per se than by exposure to intense conflict." She is joined by Melissa Ludtke, who suggests that in many instances "one parent is better than two." Yes, youngsters will not fare well if their homes are nothing but a battleground. But what writers like these want to convey is that there are many more such marriages than most people think. In this depiction, mothers leave marriages to save the children from clashes fomented by their fathers. They argue there are enough of these situations to put a positive face on divorce.

Holding quite a different view are sociologists like Paul Amato and Allan Booth. In *A Generation at Risk,* they start with the fact that divorces are much more common now compared with the past. So today two thirds to three quarters of the dissolutions end what they call "low-conflict" marriages. Such quarrels that occur in these homes are usual in families, and youngsters learn to accept them. But when told that their parents are going to part, these children are given a burden they will carry for the rest of their lives.

Some children, for example, become convinced that the divorce is their fault, an onus as cruel as it is unfair. And they often have their loyalties strained, as when they are asked by one parent to report on the doings of the other. Put very simply, a grave reduction in the overall happiness of our nation's children has occurred, due to the decisions of their parents to divorce. About the only positive factor is these children are no longer experiencing this trauma in isolation; rather, they have friends and classmates who are going through the same thing. This has led Nicholas Wolfinger, a University of Utah sociologist, to say, "Divorce will always be hard on kids; it's just not nearly as hard on them as it used to be." Indeed, in time, what they undergo may become a new norm.

The time seems right for an aside. Since social scientists belong to the middle class, they find it easier to study people from backgrounds similar to their own. This may be why they focus on how children are affected by divorce, since it is terrain they find familiar, either through their own experience or that of friends or relatives. But they have much less to tell us about youngsters whose parents never married, and who may have never known the man who helped in his or her creation. How, for example, is a child affected by having a father who essentially doesn't exist? True, most know who he is, and some see him from time to time. But for others he is a phantom presence, who even though absent will always be a part of their lives. And this kind of injury may be at least as wounding as the impact of divorce.

MANAGING WITHOUT MOMS

If more women are becoming single parents, the same is true for men. In 1970, single fathers accounted for 10.8 percent of adults raising children on their own. By 2000, this figure had almost doubled, to 20.7

percent. The number of children living only with their fathers also rose, although not as steeply, from 1.8 percent to 2.5 percent.

There are several reasons for these cases. Many will recall the 1979 movie *Kramer vs. Kramer,* a comedy with a cutting edge. Meryl Streep, feeling stifled as a full-time wife and mother, walks out and leaves her son with a hapless Dustin Hoffman. The script made no effort to show her any sympathy; indeed, she was portrayed as selfish and irresponsible. While increased opportunities for women in the workplace and elsewhere were much in the air at that time, these freedoms were not supposed to be exercised at the expense of a child. In fact, the *Kramer* scenario wasn't very typical, since decamping mothers tend to be an exception. And when this does happen, the men almost always remarry, as a sequel to the movie would surely have shown. Indeed, the plot is ready for prime time: deserted dad begins the dating game. ("Eddie's Father," from an earlier television era, was a widower; so there was no woman to blame.)

A more common reason why a father is raising the children is that the mother is mentally ill, or addicted to alcohol or drugs. Women are more apt to succumb to mental illness, sometimes precipitated by the birth and strains of child care. Regarding the use of drugs and alcohol, we have no firm figures; but some statistics offer a few clues. For example, among intoxicated drivers who cause fatal accidents, 26.8 percent are women. While men are the main culprits, the number of women involved is not negligible and it suggests there may be more heavy drinking than is often supposed. A National Institute of Justice study of persons arrested in the twenty-two largest cities found that women were more likely than men to test positive for cocaine and heroin. True, many of the women were selling sex, an occupation where narcotics bring a form of escape. In general, though, it is illusory to assume that women, including those with children, are better able than men to avoid precarious pursuits.

There are also instances where the mother takes up with a new boyfriend who specifies that he will only move in with her if she finds another place for her children. There have always been women who fall for such men. Even more depressing is how many accept their ultimatum. In other cases, the women aren't earning enough to support their children, so they're sent to live with their father. As was shown earlier in this chapter, the median income of single mothers is only $19,934, and that includes all the child support payments they receive. Only one out of five makes as much as $35,000, while half the custodial fathers earn that much.

A 2000 Census survey of children living with their fathers found that boys made up somewhat over half—56.5 percent—of that group. When boys get into their teens, some parents agree it would be better for them to live with their father. If more of them were on speaking terms, or just in contact with each other, the figure might well be higher. As it turns out, not all of the single fathers are entirely on their own. Many already have a woman residing with them or a girlfriend who may live elsewhere but is around much of the time so they are not literally single. (A table in a 2000 Census report has figures showing that single fathers are 71.7 percent more likely to have such companions than single mothers.) Nor do men who are raising children find a lack of women willing to become their wives. On the contrary, custodial fathers who do diapering and show up for school meetings come across as having traits that would make them attractive mates.

Judith Wallerstein, a psychotherapist and the author of *The Unexpected Legacy of Divorce,* estimates that among adults under the age of 45, one in four had parents who divorced. Among the coming generation of children, the proportion will be considerably higher. Wallerstein tracked some 130 youngsters, from childhood to adulthood, to uncover the effects of seeing one's parents part. One of her findings was that two thirds of the men and women she studied decided not to have children, in part because they didn't feel they could do the job well, and were fearful of putting more young people through what they had experienced. And overall, fewer adults are becoming parents compared with the past. Back in 1970, among couples where one or both were in their late thirties, only 8.5 percent had not had a child. In 2000, looking at the same group, 15.8 percent were still childless, and the likelihood is that most of them will have only one child or none. The next chapter will explore further causes for this decline.

4

Passing on Parenthood

Are children going out of style? Not altogether. But by many measures, having them is being displaced by other interests and activities. To be sure, most American women still say they want to become mothers and a majority surely will. Even so, the number who never have has reached an all-time high. A 2000 Census study of women who had reached their forties found that almost one in five had not had a child, and the likelihood is that most of them never will.* When a cross section of women were asked how many children they thought they might have, 21.3 percent answered they didn't anticipate having any at all. And those who become mothers are having smaller families. In 1970, among women in their early forties, 53.4 percent had already had three or more children. Among women currently that age, only 27.8 percent have had that many. Indeed, three-child households are becoming increasingly rare. And among couples starting out, current projections are that even more will be stopping at one.

Despite many reports in newspapers and television, declines in fertility are becoming common around the globe. A broad array of countries, ranging from Latvia and Portugal to Barbados and Singapore, have rates below replacement levels. Among the least fecund are Spain and Italy, despite their Catholic histories. Ireland and Malta also have subzero growth, even though they ban abortion and limit access to reliable contraception. Islands like Mauritius and Martinique are reproducing at less than replacement levels, signaling that successive

---

* Of the 1,622,404 first births to women in 2000, only 20,096—or 1.2 percent—were to mothers aged forty or over.

FERTILITY RATES: HERE AND ABROAD

Average Lifetime Births per 100 Women
(Needed for Replacement: 211)

Within the United States

1960	365	White	188
1970	248	Asian	207
1980	184	Black	226
1990	208	Puerto Rican	258
2000	213	Mexican	327

Abroad

High Rates		Low Rates	
Yemen	760	Canada	158
Uganda	710	Japan	133
Afghanistan	680	Sweden	129
Congo	670	Poland	126
Madagascar	586	Greece	124
Saudi Arabia	554	Italy	120
Pakistan	508	Hong Kong	117
Iraq	477	Russia	114
Nepal	448	Spain	113
Guatemala	441	Bulgaria	110

Figures are for 2000, unless otherwise noted.

births are no longer demanded by custom or family and social pressures. In all these countries, having a child is increasingly a choice, and it is one that fewer of their citizens are making. Yet places like Singapore and Martinique are not exactly feminist strongholds, and women there are only beginning to enter professional careers. Still, it is clear that there and elsewhere, decisions by individual women are changing the contours of the world's population. True, it will be some years before Yemen and Uganda get to zero growth. But if it can happen in Cyprus and Azerbaijan, as it has, the possibility should not be dismissed.

In fact, as the table on the last page showed, the United States does not have a particularly low ranking on the fertility tables. And while its rate has been declining, it has not been as precipitous as in other countries. In 1960, at the peak of the baby boom, every 100 American women would average 365 children over their lifetimes, which was greater than India's is today. However, by 1976, America's fertility rate had plummeted to 174, down to less than half the 1960 level and about the current rate for Kazakhstan. But since then, unlike in other countries, America's rate has been edging upward. It now stands at 213, about the same as Brazil's, and just over the 211 births per 100 women which is the zero-growth replacement ratio.

One reason for the recent surge in fertility has been the just discussed rise in out-of-wedlock births, which now account for one in three American infants. In past years, the out-of-wedlock rate was lower, and more women were having abortions. In 1970, for example, no one would have predicted that a resurgence in births would be led by unmarried women. Of equal importance has been the steady growth of the Hispanic population as a whole, whose rate of 311 children per 100 women has it providing one in five of the nation's births. Among Hispanics, Mexican-Americans top the fertility list at 327, which is notably higher than Mexico's 249. Americans of European ancestry, whose rate is now 188 per 100 women, supply only 58.2 percent of the current newborns. In fact, 1971 was the last year white Americans produced enough children to replenish their race.

In largest measure, the curtailing of births are women's decisions. After all, it isn't easy—at least in the United States—for a man to start a pregnancy against a woman's will. (While the incidence of rape remains high, as will be discussed in a later chapter, extremely few of these assaults result in births.) Nor are there indications that husbands and partners want to father more children. On the contrary, the sexes have much the same reasons for wanting smaller households, and in this respect there is no mismatch between women and men. While couples can and do discuss births, she now has the ultimate say, which cannot help but affect the balance of power between the sexes. This shift will be explored toward the end of this chapter.

KINDERFEINDLICHKEIT

Whether or not he said it, W. C. Fields will be remembered for snarling, "Anyone who hates children and dogs can't be all bad." And the German language has a word for it: *Kinderfeindlichkeit*. But Americans are supposed to love children, and most will say they do. Simple observation—from shopping malls to television programming—suggests that youngsters are getting an inordinate amount of attention. Still, as has been noted, more adults are passing on parenthood than ever in the past, or at least cutting back on the number of children they have. And the men and women who do become parents now spend less time with the creatures they create, whether due to parents' work schedules or fathers who move out and away.

It's probably too much to say that we are witnessing a revolt against children. What has happened, though, is that some adults are reacting against what they see as preferential treatment for parents. In their view, provisions in tax laws, health plans, and company policies end up compelling those without children to subsidize the ones who choose to reproduce. They are active in a ChildFree Network, with a Web site called *No Kidding.* Among its proposals is a Childfree Adult Day, on the first Sunday in June, halfway between Mother's Day and Father's Day. In the vision of Elinor Burkett, one of its leaders, adults who prefer their own company should be free to "shop, dine, or swim without being drowned out by wailing infants or rammed into by rambunctuous toddlers." At supermarkets, they would like to "push their carts through the aisles without having to maneuver around a bunch of six-year-olds playing hide-and-seek behind the cereal."

If this sounds like a fringe view, it should be added that it's not only adults without children who harbor a dim view of youngsters. A few years ago, a study by the Advertising Council funded by the McDonald's chain asked 4,500 adults, most of whom were parents, for their judgments on the nation's children. While the report's title, *Kids These Days,* lacked an exclamation mark, the responses expressed exasperation. Most of those who were interviewed saw today's youngsters as a problem, too long out of control. "Kids always want more," one Denver resident complained. "It's 'I want, I want, I want.'" Another Coloradan added, "Kids are not held accountable for what they do, and there are no consequences." This summation by a New Jersey man seemed to echo what others were thinking:

> By the time they are in high school, most of them are in trouble. They might not be in criminal trouble, but they are out there aggravating the neighborhoods and raising hell in the streets.

Altogether, 71.0 percent said they usually saw young people "out of control in public areas such as restaurants and the movies," while 74.0 percent felt it "common" that children are "lazy and do not apply themselves," and 84.6 percent believe today's youngsters are "spoiled and do not appreciate what they have."

The report's subtitle was revealing. Its manner of phrasing, *What Americans Really Think About the Next Generation,* suggested that the adults who were responding regarded young people as an alien nation. Nowhere was it said that these "kids" who will be the "next generation" were conceived and raised and often still resided in homes headed by the very adults whose judgments were being solicited and reported.

IS BEING CHILDLESS SELFISH?

Not so very long ago, adults who chose not to have children were accused of being selfish. If the charge is not heard as much today, the sentiment behind it has not wholly disappeared. There's an enduring belief that people must procreate to perpetuate a family or faith, to strengthen their nation, even ensure the survival of the species. And in much of the world, the command to be fruitful and multiply is still pronounced and heeded. But despite these appeals, far fewer people than in the past believe they have an obligation to become parents.

There are individuals and couples who have decided either singly or jointly that their lives will be more enjoyable and productive if they are not encumbered by children. We might start by asking if their choice brings harm to anyone. In fact, it is difficult to show that it does. Even if some childless adults are self-absorbed, whether as individuals or in pairs, forgoing parenthood need not mean they are taking more from the world than they are contributing to it. Indeed, what they add may be more creative, since they have not had to expend time and energy on childrearing.

Granted, they are not helping to produce the next generation. However, it is not clear that the globe needs as many people as it has. On the contrary, there is a strong case for scaling back from our current 6 billion. Nor is the problem just finding food for those in less-developed countries, which is where birthrates are the highest. Equally critical are the ravenous appetites of the more comfortable classes in the first world. Since the children now being born in these places will devour more of the world's resources, having fewer births will slow the exhaustion of the planet. That said, there is at least one reason why size matters for the next generation, at least in this country. Given the way our retirement systems are set up, pensions will largely depend on the wealth that tomorrow's workers will produce and the taxes they will pay. And someone will have to be on hand to service the elderly, especially in assisted-living facilities and nursing homes.

Childless adults might respond that they are paying plenty of taxes, which are used to educate other people's offspring, among other things. And if the country faces shortages of labor for certain kinds of work—as it already does—there is no dearth of immigrants ready to take on those jobs. Moreover, these newcomers bring a vitality and ambition, renewing the nation's vigor. And at least part of what spurs them on is a drive to create opportunities for their own children.

Economists like to talk about the "opportunity cost" of any human endeavor. Put simply, if you make a certain choice, then you forgo enjoyments or experiences that another decision might have brought.

It is easy to see how this kind of calculation applies to becoming a parent. Elaborating on this theme, Nathan Keyfitz, a Canadian demographer, begins by asking, *"Is childrearing work or pleasure?"* He suggests that increasing numbers of adults are saying that the labor is not matched by a sufficient payoff:

> Childrearing as an activity is less able to compete in attractiveness with . . . the pleasure of alternative activities in this exciting world of consumption. . . . Air travel, living in hotels, eating in restaurants, are all handicapped by the presence of children. The child as a product is of insufficient value to the parents to cause them to give up alternative commodities.

So let's grant that over the years, childless individuals and couples enjoy more travel, spend more evenings out, and spend more time conversing with adults, than do those who decide to have and raise children. But is this evidence that persons who choose parenthood are getting less out of life?

One way to continue the conversation is to consider whether procreation should be regarded as an altruistic act. In fact, men and women who make this choice do so because they believe it will bring more pleasure to themselves than would otherwise be the case. Of course, there are no guarantees, as it is impossible to predict whether children will turn out to be disappointing. On the whole, though, most who have taken on parenthood will attest that its benefits outweighed the drawbacks and they would do it again. And they might add that those gains were greater than whatever else might have happened had they not had children.

"QUALITY CHILDREN"

In the past, children were welcomed as more hands to work the farm. If parents today stop at one or two offspring, it is because they hope to improve the "quality" of these youngsters' lives. True, parents in earlier times wanted their progeny to be at least moderately successful, so they could care for them in their old age. But it's more difficult to quantify the expected returns of children today, since modern parents are less apt to look to them for economic support. Instead, they do all they can to ensure that their children will have visible achievements, with praise accruing to the parents as a fringe benefit. Acceptance by an elite college is an obvious example, as is entry into a recognized profession. So it isn't clear that parents' decisions to invest in their children should deserve praise, let alone be described as selfless or altruistic.

If parents curtail their enjoyments to aid their offspring, should they be lauded for making sacrifices? In earlier times, a mother took in laundry and a father worked a second shift so their children could go to college. True, in a literal sense, those parents gave up some things in order to achieve others. But the overriding point is that their choices were made willingly, whether in hopes of acclaim from others or simply to feel that they had done their best to help their children realize their potential. In short, there are no grounds for regarding becoming a parent as "altruistic," nor should anything adults do to aid their offspring be seen as a "sacrifice."

Kathleen Gerson, a sociologist at New York University, found refreshing candor among the women she interviewed for her oft-cited study, *Hard Choices: How Women Decide About Work, Careers, and Motherhood.* Here are a few examples:

> Little babies aren't what people tell you they will be. There's isn't a whole hell of a lot you can do with a child four or five months old.
> I tried staying home six months. I was ready for the looney farm.
> Staying home was not for me. I loved my children dearly, and I loved my husband dearly. But I wasn't going to sacrifice my life for these individuals.
> I've never been interested in children. I'm really scared of kids, scared of the responsibility, scared of what I could do to their minds, to their lives.

These comments are revealing. The first woman confesses that she isn't one for being with babies, but hints she might find them agreeable later on. The second says she loves her children, but would prefer to limit her mothering to weekends and evenings. The third woman is thoroughly honest about herself. She might even have remarked that she looked forward to being a model *aunt,* serving as a third parent and confidante to her nephews and nieces. Many childless adults fill such a role with aplomb, expanding the boundaries in a youngster's upbringing.

In the past, some women did circumvent social and parental pressure to marry and have children. Two groups, from markedly different backgrounds, come to mind. One included graduates of top-ranked women's colleges through the first half of the last century. Students there were taught that they had minds and talents that should be dedicated to serious purposes. Alumnae of Bryn Mawr, Wellesley, and their sister colleges pioneered in varied professions, in numbers not matched until many decades later. To some degree, they were inspired by their professors, most of whom were single. These were attractive young women, many of whom received marriage proposals from suitors at schools like Princeton and Yale. But they turned them down. They knew what they wanted to make of their lives, and it was not to end up as matronly wives of bankers and brokers.

At about the same time, America's cities were teeming with the offspring of Irish immigrants. Most of their daughters wed early. And since contraception was a sin, six or seven children followed in quick succession. But some young women were repelled by the prospect of domestic drudgery, and didn't want to look 50 by the time they reached 30, with their husbands installed at the corner pub. So they made the hard choice of spinsterhood. A few chose religious vocations. But many more became the Miss Kellys and Miss O'Briens who educated the next generation of youngsters in the cities' public schools. In an important sense they did "have" children. After all, millions of adults would later recall the imprint that the Miss Kellys had made on their lives.

People who in the past would have become parents at earlier ages are now choosing to do other things with their lives. This new generation is better educated, at least in terms of years of schooling. They see themselves as more sophisticated, with longer lists of interests and activities. As a result, they are postponing marriage, if they embark on it at all. From 1970 to 2000, the average age of grooms rose from 23 to 27, while for brides it went from 20 to 25. This leaves a shorter span for having children, at least within marriage. As the table on this page shows, in 1970, fully 81.2 percent of first births were to mothers under 25, almost all of whom were married. Today, only 51.8 percent of first births are to mothers under this age, and close to half of these are to unmarried women.

Some of the most striking changes have been among educated women, most of whom view their schooling as an investment that should be protected. In 1970, as the table also shows, almost three quarters of college women had given birth while they were still in their twenties, and for most of them that meant leaving what might have been promising careers. By 2000, only 36.6 percent were starting babies that early, and many of them had arranged to return to their job. Also in 1970, among women graduates who were in their forties, only

AGE OF MOTHERS AT BIRTH OF FIRST BABY

1970	All Women	2000
81.2%	Under 25	51.8%
14.8%	25–29	24.3%
3.0%	30–34	16.5%
1.0%	Over 34	7.4%
100.0%		100.0%

1970	College Graduates	2000
22.4%	Under 25	5.6%
50.5%	25–29	31.0%
20.4%	30–34	39.5%
6.7%	Over 34	23.9%
100.0%		100.0%

9.5 percent hadn't yet had a child. Thirty years later, the childless proportion at that age had tripled to 28.6 percent.

NATURE AND NATALISM

It isn't easy today to appreciate how ingrained ideologies about childbearing dominated this country not many decades ago. Human reproduction, like that of other creatures, was seen as governed by Darwinian imperatives. In fact, the voluntary curbing of births is a relatively new development, and one that counters theories about how species seek to ensure their survival. In that view, all strive to create yet another generation bearing their genes. Both men and women are said to possess this drive, with each sex seeking to attract mates having the hardiest features.

Women were told that a "maternal instinct" was part of their makeup. After all, nature had given them a capacity for bearing children; to fail to use it would be untrue to their essential selves. To underscore this point, consider the words of two professors of psychiatry, at illustrious institutions, written in the 1960s. The first pronouncement was by Joseph Rheingold, of Harvard University; the second came from Bruno Bettelheim, at the University of Chicago:

> We must start with the realization that, as much as women want to be good scientists and engineers, they want first and foremost to be womenly companions of men and to be mothers.

> Anatomy decrees the life of a woman . . . When women grow up without dread of their biological functions and without subversion by feminist doctrine, and therefore enter upon motherhood with a sense of fulfillment and altruistic sentiment, we shall attain the goal of a good life and a secure world in which to live it.

The thrust of these statements is that having children stems not from a conscious choice, but from drives within women that insist on being expressed. Interestingly, this kind of anatomical determinism was never applied to men. True, fewer of their organs engage in reproductive functions. Even so, sexual stirrings are strong urges in men's lives, and they can lead to conceptions. But does their presence signify, to paraphrase Professor Rheingold, that all *men* "want first and foremost to be fathers"? In the past, one might make such a case. Even today, in countries and cultures that are closer to their patriarchic origins, it remains a point of pride for a man to sire many children. But now, in all corners of the globe, fewer men are using this route to ratify their manhood.

When the two professors issued their edicts, they spoke for an establishment dominated by men, who felt entitled to lecture women on the lives they were fated to lead. As is often the case, what they were propounding was not science, but rather *ideology:* doctrines intended to preserve the primacy of one group, while relegating another to subordination. Ascertaining what comes *naturally* to the respective sexes is still contentious terrain. Indeed, there are few if any findings on which scientists can agree. Still, a sign of how far the discussion has moved is that incantations to be *"womanly companions of men"* are seldom heard today. And this is not simply because they are embarrassing. Rather, we now are less sure of our knowledge in this sphere; but at least know enough not to mount sweeping assertions about an entire sex.

For understandable reasons, most of the analysis of declining births has focused on women. What has received little comment is that today's men are less inclined toward fatherhood than was once the case. For one thing, there seems to be less sentiment about perpetuating a family name, with the premium it placed on having sons. In fact, many parents now regard their daughters and sons as equals. Evidence of this will emerge in the next chapter, which deals with education. For the moment, we may recall what happened when men's colleges in the Ivy League decided to admit women. The idea originated with professors, who felt that mingling the sexes in the classroom would enhance the academic interchange. But there were worries at Yale and Dartmouth and other schools that their all-male alumni would try to veto the proposals. In fact, few if any objections were heard. It turned out that these men wanted their daughters to go to the colleges they had attended. And today you can hear them boasting about how their girls are doing at Merrill Lynch and Mobil-Exxon and Harvard Medical School.

THE COSTS OF CHILDREN

By all accounts, it costs more to raise children than in the past. Even items like sneakers have expensive high-tech features. Youngsters rooms' are crammed with electronic equipment, just as trips to Disney playlands must be factored into family budgets. Each year, the Department of Agriculture estimates the cost of raising a child from birth through age eighteen. For those born in 1970, the outlay averaged $140,965 in today's dollars. For those born in 2000, the cost will be $233,530 over eighteen years, about two thirds higher. This meant that the total dollars spent on rearing a child born in 1970 worked out to be 3.6 times the median family income for that year. Expenditures on a typical child born in 2000 will end up absorbing 5.1 times its family's annual income.

Nor do the expenses end when children reach eighteen. In fact, the largest single expenditure, for parents who undertake it, is to send their offspring through college. Over half of high school graduates now continue their education, although some of them go to community colleges and not all who enroll finish. Still, in recent years, some 1.2 million Americans annually have been receiving bachelor's degrees, and usually parents pay the bulk of the bills.

True, about two thirds of students go to public colleges. Yet even there charges are no longer nominal. In-state students at the University of Michigan in 2002 paid $8,248 for tuition, while the bill at New Hampshire is $8,130, to which must be added travel, room and board, social activities, and forgone earnings. And among the nation's 1,705 private colleges, fully 40 percent are asking over $16,000 for tuition alone. Many are schools with regional reputations; Hiram College in Ohio, to cite one example, was charging $19,650 a year for a classroom seat. In fact, parents willingly write checks and students take out loans, because a degree brings financial dividends, and also it signals your middle-class—even upper-middle-class—status.

REGRESSING TO THE MEAN?

So why do people have children? One motive, certainly, is to prove to yourself and the world what a fine parent you can be. This endeavor begins with the belief that your child will carry the best of your genes. Most adults are quite pleased with the kind of people they are, even if they feel their qualities are not fully appreciated by the wider world. Hence the hope that passing on your traits and aptitudes will produce a superior child, and you will be able to share in the acclaim he or she receives.

After conception and birth, parents are expected to transform a howling infant into a motivated adolescent and an accomplished college applicant. Most also want their children to make more of their lives than they have themselves. Thus much of parenthood involves devising a game plan to ensure that one's child will surpass his or her schoolmates. This includes spending large sums of money on lessons and activities associated with winning, ranging from music and sports, computing and martial arts, along with efforts to get the child into advanced placement classes and programs for pupils identified as gifted. Indeed, the main reason for migrations to the suburbs is to send children to schools that will serve as springboards to recognized colleges and a higher social status.

In a word, parenthood has become a competition. If some children are deemed winners, others are seen as losers, even if that term is seldom uttered aloud. For example, a dozen elite colleges listed in the next chapter had only 15,577 freshmen places in 2000, not nearly enough for all the parents who want to say that their Jennifer is at Duke and Jason is at Stanford. The public sector is almost as selective. In California, Berkeley rejected 21,599 of its 30,042 applicants, while UCLA turned down 25,385 out of 35,681. In North Carolina, its flagship campus at Chapel Hill mailed 6,178 admission letters and 10,635 expressing regrets. Investments in private schooling or well-off suburban systems can't be said to have paid off if one's offspring end up at lower-tier colleges whose names aren't quite as impressive.

Part of the problem is that demand exceeds supply by a wide margin. The United States now has a larger upper-middle class than ever in its history. In 2000, the Internal Revenue Service received returns that reported incomes of at least $100,000 from 10,856,126 households. While not all had college-age children, some did and they were among the losing competitors for Dartmouth and Berkeley and Chapel Hill.

So what happens when children do not succeed? When asked what a son or daughter is doing—and people do ask—here is what some not-wholly-fictional parents may find themselves saying:

> He's a carpenter up in Vermont, and he's really happy and he says he's truly found himself.
>
> It's a small liberal arts college in Indiana, which has excellent internship programs.
>
> She's building a good life for herself and the girls, now that her ex is out of the house.

One cannot miss the tone: plaintive, defensive, embarrassed. By middle-class American measures, these children are—not to mince words—failures. And the fault must lie with the parents, whether through inadequate genes or insufficient encouragement. "Where did they go wrong?" they feel others asking—and they may be asking themselves the same question. So they work on how they'll respond, as others hold forth on their neurosurgeon sons and investment banker daughters.

What is being described here is the side of social mobility that is seldom discussed. For most escalators that move upward, there will be another one going down. Even in prosperous periods, when the majority of society is doing well, there will be children who sink below the status they enjoyed while growing up. After all, even the best-placed parents cannot guarantee that their energy and intellect will be passed on. A suburban education may get a child into Princeton, but after that she'll be on her own. Many Ivied graduates end up with middling jobs, and then find themselves replaced by more talented men and women from less auspicious origins. This process has been called *"regression to the mean,"* wherein offspring of successful parents turn out to be quite average in character and accomplishment. This can happen even in favored families; indeed, that's where it usually occurs.

GOING IT ALONE

Another deterrent to parenthood is characteristic of our time: there is a concern about being a "good parent." In the past, parents had an extended support system. Three generations of a family would live near one another in a rural county or an urban area, where they worshiped together and shared common celebrations. Today, fewer and fewer families have such a network that was once taken for granted. Adult brothers and sisters are typically scattered across the country, visiting only intermittently, while young children see their grandparents only several days a year.

One result is that adults who now embark on parenthood are essentially on their own. During the baby boom years, most mothers were in the home. Even if in transient suburbs, women would exchange sympathy and support in car pools, over coffee, and in school associations. (A well-thumbed copy of *Dr. Spock* provided down-to-earth advice.) Today, with both parents often working, mothers see as little of their children as fathers usually have. And since most of these men and women are urbane and educated, they assume that *parenting* has experts and authorities, whose research and insights should be known and heeded. So replacing *Dr. Spock* are the endless volumes that pack bookstore shelves, filled with manuals and guides for every phase of a youngster's life and every anxiety that may arise in a parent's head. These volumes of advice prompt the surmise that when faced with raising the children they have created, today's adults have less confidence about themselves than did earlier and less literate generations. And this may result, directly or indirectly, in their deciding to take a pass on having children.

PARTIAL PARENTHOOD

Between 1970 and 2000, the number of married couples with children stayed essentially the same, actually dipping slightly from from 25,406,000 to 25,248,000. And this was during a period when the total population rose by 37.2 percent. More than that, while the country was growing, the number of children living with their two biological parents dropped dramatically, from 58,939,000 to 49,795,000. So relative to the population, fewer Americans are married parents, and they are having fewer children, and more youngsters are being born to single parents and are being raised by them.

What we are witnessing here are the outcomes of millions of decisions, most of which, as previously mentioned, are being made by women. To be sure, the choice can be preceded by discussions, involving husbands or other potential fathers. Still, the decision to bear a child or not, or to have more than one, rests ultimately with the woman. At issue, then, is what underlies the resolve to have fewer children or do without them altogether. Whether they reside in the United States or Hong Kong or Bulgaria, women want a lot more from life than being homemakers and mothers. And even if they have a husband and a child, they don't expect these relationships to be all-consuming. More of them are pursuing careers that call for longer hours at their places of employment, out-of-town travel, and bringing work home. For those who are married, this was part of an implied contract to which their husbands consented. Hence the need for nannies and housekeepers and child care arrangements, accompanied by increasing demands that public funds should pay some of these bills. More than ever, ours has become an era of partial parenthood.

What ends up bothering at least some of these men is not their family's bypassing parenthood, but the feeling that they are being neglected themselves. No, they don't want a fully domesticated wife; they're much too modern for that. And by all outward indications, they show pride in their wife's professional success. Still, times arise when a man finds himself wondering whether his wife's choice to have fewer children—or none at all—is also part of a package where less attention is accorded to him. On occasions like these, he may begin to fantasize about not a larger brood, but perhaps a companion who is less committed to interests with which he cannot readily identify.

At this point the sociologists weigh in. According to Alan Booth and Paul Amato, whose studies were cited earlier, "analysis has shown that employment among married women is a significant predictor of the divorce rate," and that "couples with employed wives report thinking about divorce more." Stacy Rogers of Pennsylvania State University cites research showing that "wives' income negatively affects marriage by threatening spouses' role complementarity." More simply stated, many husbands have their self-assurance shaken when their wives bank paychecks of their own. And Susan Crohan, who teaches at Wheelock College in Boston, found that "spouses who become parents report lower marital happiness and more frequent conflicts," in large part because working wives feel stuck with an unfair share of attending to the children and other chores.

If many husbands are disconcerted by the full implications of partial parenthood, so are many wives. In their initial compact, the husband said he wanted both of them to develop their talents fully and equally, without cavils or reservations. But now he has begun to sound more like his father. As his spouse sees it, the quarrels are not really about who spends how much *time* doing what, although that is not unimportant. Rather they concern the respect he has for her as an individual, and her desire to create a fulfilling life. If he can't show that, then she finds herself wondering if he is the man she once thought he was and if she wants to continue living with him.

This chapter has considered the cost of going to college and why parents set so much store on their children receiving degrees. The chapter that follows will show how their offspring have been faring, from early grades through graduate school. What will be detailed is how in classrooms and seminars, women are moving ahead while men are dropping out. So another mismatch is in the making, as fewer men share the education and interests that are accruing to women.

5

Education:
The Case of the Missing Men

Arguing over whether men or women are smarter is bound to be a fruitless enterprise. Each sex has its share of geniuses and fools, each has varied strengths and shortcomings, just as individuals can be clever and creative in innumerable ways. Brilliance may be expressed by devising mathematical theorems or playing the cello, through inspiring troops in battle or creating new cuisines, even in a flair for friendship or in teaching reading to young children. There are as many modes of intelligence and insight as there are human endeavors.

With these caveats noted, the pages that follow will focus in on measuring mental abilities, at least as practiced in the world we know. This occurs mainly in organized education, where grades and scores are recorded from kindergarten through graduate school. One of the hallmarks of our time is to assign numerical evaluations to almost everything in sight, from beauty contestants to restaurants. But the stakes are higher in schooling, where the aim is to bring out the best in young minds. So, as the statistics roll in, we must always ask what the tests claim to measure and whether in fact they are accomplishing what they set out to do.

WHY GIRLS GET BETTER GRADES

Women are better students. In classrooms, they surpass men at almost every age and in most parts of the curriculum. The most visible exception is mathematics, where boys begin to move ahead in the final year of high school. Yet even there, their lead may have less to do with the subject than with how mathematical competence is tested.

Of course, not all women excel at school. But more of them do than men, as is revealed by several measures. Among the high school seniors who took the 2000 Scholastic Assessment Test, 43.7 percent of the girls had A averages, compared with 35.4 percent of the boys. And they take their assignments more seriously. Among female high school seniors, 74.1 percent devote at least an hour each day to their homework, compared with 57.4 percent of the boys. In fact, boys start getting distracted at an early stage. By fourth grade, 22.4 percent of them watch television six or more hours daily, notably higher than the 15.5 percent of girls who spend that much time in front of the tube. By the time they become seniors, 19.2 percent of the boys devote an hour or more each day to video games, against 6.8 percent of the girls. (They may spend more time chatting on the telephone, but thus far no one has clocked their rate.)

As it happens, the advances of girls and women are relatively recent, reflecting the expanded opportunities open to them and their readiness to take advantage of these options. For example, not so very long ago, in 1987, boys outnumbered girls in most high school advanced placement courses. This ratio and others have been reversed. For every 100 boys now in those programs, there are 124 girls, just as academic honor societies are selecting 158 girls for every 100 boys. In outside activities like yearbook and newspaper staffs, girls outnumber boys by a factor of 169 to 100.

Given their academic achievements, it is not surprising that more women attend college. In 2000, they made up 53.7 percent of those who sat for the SAT, and 56.8 percent taking the ACT, the two tests required by selective schools. As can be seen in the table on the next page, they now receive 57.2 percent of all bachelor's degrees, and almost half of the doctorates granted to American citizens. In the eight professional fields, their ascent has been steady, and in two—pharmacy and veterinary medicine—they have all but eclipsed the men.

Moreover, the proportion of college graduates who are men has been declining in all ethnic groups. Among black students, they now receive only 35.1 percent of all bachelor's degrees, while white men account for 44.3 percent of their race's total. It was once assumed that Hispanic and Asian cultures favored their men and paid scant atten-

BACHELORS AND OTHERS

Proportions of Degrees Awarded to Women

	BAs	PhDs	Medicine
1960	38.5%	10.5%	5.5%
1970	43.1%	13.3%	8.4%
1980	49.0%	29.7%	23.4%
2000	57.2%	48.9%*	42.7%

	Law	MBAs	Engineers
1960	2.5%	3.6%	0.4%
1970	5.4%	3.6%	0.8%
1980	30.2%	22.4%	9.3%
2000	45.9%	39.8%	20.4%

	Dentists	Pharmacy	Veterinary
1960	0.8%	12.4%	NA
1970	0.9%	18.2%	5.8%
1980	13.3%	40.0%	36.2%
2000	40.1%	65.7%	68.5%

*2000 figure omits PhDs awarded to foreign students.

tion to women's education. If that was once the case, it no longer is. Asian women now get 53.4 percent of their group's undergraduate degrees, and the share for Hispanic women is 58.1 percent.

SEVENTEEN YEARS OF SITTING

Teachers can tell you why girls are more academically adept, and many of the explanations offered here are based on my own years in the classroom. For one thing, formal education rests on a specified structure of learning, and students are expected to adhere to the regimen. Girls and women have a subtler understanding of authority. (When you have less power, it is prudent to understand how the system works.) Very early, they come to understand that academic success depends on adult evaluations. So they become skilled at intuiting what teachers want, heeding instructions that accompany tests and assignments. Boys are more apt to listen with half an ear, already framing what they want to say. Teachers will tell you that in examinations calling for essays, boys usually begin writing right away, while girls spend more time thinking about how to organize their answers.

Girls are neater and more punctual. Many tests and worksheets are still submitted in longhand, and girls' writing tends to be more legible, just as the notes they take for class or homework are better organized. Among those who turn in assignments late, boys outnumber girls by a considerable margin. When it is optional, or suggested rather than required, girls are more likely to do the work. For some, the motive may be to please the teacher and obtain a higher grade. But others put in the extra effort because they want to learn more about the subject. They also tend to be more at home with ambiguity and uncertainty, more tolerant of imprecise boundaries and indeterminate shadings. Girls are also more reluctant to come to quick conclusions, an inclination that does not always serve them well, especially in an age of quickly paced tests.

Education, certainly through high school, is staffed largely by women and bears their imprint. The 2001 count by the Bureau of Labor Statistics found that women made up 97.8 percent of nursery and kindergarten teachers, 82.5 percent of elementary teachers, and now are a majority—58.5 percent—of high school faculty. Each year more are appointed as principals and superintendents. Although they account for less than half—43.3 percent—of all college staffs, they predominate among instructors and adjuncts, who teach most of the first courses that freshmen encounter.

A wag once defined education as seventeen years of sustained sitting, from kindergarten through a bachelor's degree. This assumes that students learn best when they are confined to chairs in orderly rows. It hardly needs saying that boys taken together are less suited for this regimen, which requires them to remain still and largely silent for six or more hours. So we should not be surprised when, upon being released from high school, growing numbers of young men are deciding against further confinement in college.

This is not the place to examine the ideals and illusions of academic education. For our purposes, the relevant reality is that a bachelor's degree is essentially required for middle-class occupations, and often social acceptance. (About the only career path that circumvents this rule is starting a business of your own.) Yet each year fewer men are obtaining the college credential, while the number of women doing so continues to grow. One result is that more women are among the candidates for professional positions, and are frequently chosen, not least because they have better records than many of the men. Even now, more men than ever before are being hired and fired and overseen by women supervisors.

RICH BOYS, POOR GIRLS

It is widely assumed that parents' economic status has a lot to do with who attends college. And to a large extent this is true. After all, many of the very poor never finish high school, while well-off families usually find a college that will take even their least academically oriented offspring. But what is less known is that the link between family income and attending college differs for the two sexes. This becomes evident if we examine the finances of the families whose 419,196 sons and 507,798 daughters took the SAT in 2000.

As the table on the next page shows, in families in the top tier, with incomes over $100,000, boys and girls are about equally represented. This shouldn't be surprising: at that level, parents have the resources to steer all their children toward college. However, a few brackets down, at a fairly comfortable $60,000 to $80,000 income level, boys have dropped to 47.2 percent of those taking the test. They continue falling away, and when incomes are under $20,000, they account for only 37.9 percent of students on the college track. It used to be that poorer families would only send their sons to college, while the daughters went to work or got married. Today, the reverse is the case. Insofar as education is also a route to upward mobility, more women than men are taking advantage of this upward track.

At this point, two reasons can be cited for this shift. The first is that families with lower incomes are more likely to be headed by women. Sad to say, mothers raising children on their own have less sway over their sons, especially in poorer areas, where teenaged peers are a dominant influence. The Higher Education Research Institute at UCLA found that among college students from homes headed by mothers, girls outnumbered boys by a factor of 36.9 percent. A second reason was mentioned in the last chapter: fewer teenaged girls are hav-

COLLEGE-BOUND HIGH SCHOOL SENIORS

The Sexes by Brackets

Women	Family Incomes	Men
49.6%	Over $100,000	50.4%
52.0%	$80,000–$100,000	48.0%
52.9%	$60,000–$70,000	47.1%
54.7%	$40,000–$50,000	45.3%
58.7%	$20,000–$30,000	41.3%
62.1%	Under $20,000	37.9%
53.7%	All Students	46.3%

ing babies. During the decade that ended in 2000, births among them fell by 21.9 percent, and dropped for all races and income levels. This has helped to expand the pool of young women who are going on to college.

THE DOZEN

Students can obtain an outstanding education in many settings, including public institutions and those with regional reputations. That granted, the United States boasts a small group of selective colleges whose names bring instant recognition and are thought to launch their graduates on notable careers. While people can and will differ over which schools make the cut, college counselors will tell you that certain names invariably crop up. For our purposes, twelve have been chosen. The list begins with the eight from the Ivy League: Harvard, Yale, Princeton, Dartmouth, Columbia, Cornell, Brown, and the University of Pennsylvania. Another four have been added: Duke and Stanford; and two smaller colleges, Amherst and Williams.

In 2000, the dozen enrolled a total of 60,633 undergraduates. Much of the middle class, and even more of the better-off, covet these places for their children. After all, they want their offspring to have an extra edge in the arenas they will enter in later life. Acceptance at Amherst, for example, raises your odds of being admitted to Stanford Law School, which in turn means a better chance of offers from leading law firms. These dozen colleges have long been regarded as a source of recruits for the nation's most prominent positions. At the same time, in recent years there have been important changes in the composition of the pool. For one thing, it is less Caucasian and Christian. But equally striking has been a sexual shift. In 1970, women acounted for only 21.8 percent of the total number of students in the twelve; by 2000, their representation had more than doubled to just short of half. Indeed, as the table on the next page shows, women now form the majority in three of the twelve schools.

In largest measure, this change has been due to the advent of coeducation at the five colleges that in 1970 had no women at all. Since then, all of them have gone from zero women to half or close to half.

WILL THERE BE A PLACE
FOR YOUR SON AT YALE?

Percentage Women			Changes: 1970 to 2000	
1970	2000		Men	Women
-0-	48.1%	Amherst	-376	+801
28.4%	52.6%	Brown	-242	+1,855
-0-	51.2%	Columbia	-730	+2,005
37.2%	51.7%	Cornell	-84	+972
-0-	47.9%	Dartmouth	-1,161	+1,938
37.9%	48.0%	Duke	+287	+1,201
20.6%	46.3%	Harvard	-1,198	+1,853
34.5%	48.9%	Penn	-127	+1,985
11.1%	46.5%	Princeton	-775	+1,735
34.9%	49.1%	Stanford	-763	+1,032
-0-	49.0%	Williams	-300	+1,016
-0-	49.5%	Yale	-2,072	+2,601
21.8%	49.0%	All Twelve	-7,541	+18,994

Notes: Only full-time undergraduates are counted. Between 1970 and 2000, enrollments at the twelve colleges grew from 49,183 to 60,633. Cornell's count is confined to its College of Arts and Sciences. By 1970, women were fully integrated into Harvard, and at Princeton just its freshmen class had women.

But that trend also led colleges that were previously coeducational to make more places for women. Back in 1970, they purposely curtailed how many women they would admit. As can be seen on the table, Stanford and Penn set their enrollments for women at about a third; at Harvard and Brown they were even lower.

To accommodate the arrival of women, or to raise their ratio, the dozen expanded their enrollments, adding 11,450 undergraduates over the 30 years. Columbia increased its student body by 48.3 percent, and Williams grew by 52.7 percent. But others held firm: Harvard created only 655 new places, and Stanford a scant 269. Thus the key consequence of women's admissions was to displace men. By 2000, the twelve institutions together not only had 18,911 more women, but 7,541 fewer men than in 1970. Among the missing men are 1,161 who earlier would have been at Dartmouth, and another 2,072 who would have had a Yale degree had its college not embraced coeducation.

In 1970, when these schools admitted only 10,740 women, six well-regarded women's colleges provided an additional 10,350 places. At that time, it was generally presumed that a degree from Smith or Wellesley or Vassar was on a par with one from Princeton or Columbia or Cornell. Even so, women's attitudes and aspirations were changing. It soon became clear that given the chance and the choice, a new generation of women would choose to attend Williams or Yale over Mount Holyoke or Bryn Mawr. Princeton took the first step in 1970, and had no trouble finding 411 freshmen women to join its 3,235 men. By 2000, there were 29,731 women in the dozen, almost three times the total enrollment that year at the six women's schools.

As has been noted, certain men who would have once gone to Stanford and Princeton will have to settle for degrees from schools like Hamilton or Haverford. While this does not mean they are doomed to poverty, they will not have credentials that are more apt to open doors. Women who have gained admission should be pleased, especially if they feel that four years at a top school will aid not only their intellectual development but also their corporate and professional climb. But, as always, there is another side to the coin. In 1970, the women in the seven coed schools were in scarce supply. Stanford, for example, had 189 men on its campus for every 100 women. At Brown, the ratio favored women by 252 to 100, and at Harvard every 100 could

SEX AND THE SAT

All Students	Men	Women	Ratio
Verbal	507	504	99.4%
Math	533	498	93.4%

Top Tenth of High School Seniors

	Men	Women	Ratio
Verbal	593	585	98.7%
Math	634	588	92.7%

Adjusted for Parents' Income

	Men	Women	Ratio
Verbal	507	510	100.6%
Math	533	502	94.2%

Adjusted for Parents' Education

	Men	Women	Ratio
Verbal	507	519	102.4%
Math	533	504	94.4%

pick and choose among 386 men. Also, total enrollments at the all-men's schools exceeded their women's counterparts by a factor of two thirds.

By 2000, the ratios were very different. Brown had only 90 men for every 100 women; at Cornell, there ware 93. In New York's Morningside Heights complex, when Barnard's women are added to those at Columbia, the ratio became 45 men per 100 women.

Of course, people go to college to get an education. But there is also the social side, with the expectation that at least some people will be pairing off. Even in our modern era, students still go on dates, where the man usually extends an invitation and the woman chooses her response. This is why women have always wanted to be outnumbered by men. The more who may take a fancy to her, the better the odds that she will find one of them attractive. Even a 50-50 ratio. This is not to say that today's students are looking to find future wives and husbands at college. On the contrary, the majority now want a fairly long period of being single after receiving their degree. At the same time, most would like the pleasures of being in a pair. But given the recent ratios, this will be less likely for women who are continuing with higher education.

SEX AND THE SAT: DOES IT MEASURE MERIT?

Going by the published results, men do better than women on most standardized tests. On the SAT, for example, they have averaged higher scores on both the verbal and the mathematics parts for at least thirty years. Moreover, as the table on the previous page shows, women are behind even when they rank in the top tenth of their high school class.

The test has been the subject of much comment and criticism, and that scrutiny is clearly warranted. If nothing else, it's the closest thing we have to a national IQ test. Each year, some 1.3 million high school seniors take it, about one third of all Americans in their age group. The great majority of them proceed with some form of higher education. If you are a typical reader of this book, you probably took the SAT some years ago, and still recall its format. It generally has about

140 questions, which you must deal with in 180 minutes. Each item has five answers, of which four are wrong. So the student must hit on which one the testmakers have decided is correct. (Two such questions will be shown later in this chapter.)

Some teachers are convinced that the multiple-choice matrix tends to favor boys. They are more attuned to the idea that there can be only one correct answer, so they zero in on the one they've chosen and speed on to the next question. For girls, the world is much more indefinite and ambiguous. For example, they may feel that two of the five choices are appropriate, each in its own way. If they fill in both, their answer will be voided. But their more likely problem is to spend too much time pondering about their choice, so they may not have enough time to get to the questions at the end of the test.*

On first hearing, this may seem like a plausible theory. However, it's only partially correct. What must also be factored in is a disparity mentioned earlier: that the girls who take the SAT are more likely to come from lower-income homes. As a result, a larger number of them grow up in neighborhoods where schools are not as rigorous, often lacking test-preparation programs. Also, as has been noted, more of the girls live with a single parent, which is the major explanation for tighter budgets. It's as if the sexes are raised in two separate societies, with quite different income distributions.

In order to make the scores comparable, I calculated what the girls' averages might be if their families' finances matched those of the boys. My aim was to see what would happen if more of them lived in higher-bracket homes, which usually have better results. As the table shows, this adjustment lifts the girls' average on the verbal part by six points, now putting them slightly ahead. The SAT also asks the students for their parents' educational level, and here too the girls reported less schooling. Thus 51.4 percent of them had a parent with a college degree, compared with 57.4 percent of the boys. When this aspect of their environment is matched, the girls' verbal average rises

*In 2005, the SAT will add a section to the test that will require students to write a short essay. This raises questions about who will read and grade 1.3 million compositions soon enough to get the scores to college admissions offices. However, this may not turn out to be a problem, since the SAT already has scanners that can read and grade essays, using programs that judge how well they are organized.

a dozen points, even more than when incomes are equalized. Findings like these are all the more impressive since the verbal section also uses the multiple-choice format, and rigid time constraints. There is reason to believe that girls might be happier with other kinds of tests. However, they seem to have adapted to the SAT format, which they will encounter again when applying to graduate schools. And this is yet another measure of their commitment to attending college and embarking on professional careers.

MATHEMATICS: CAN WOMEN CATCH UP?

But even when social and economic conditions are evened out, the gap in mathematics scores remains basically the same. This disparity has long been subjected to debate and discussion. Women have been said to harbor a "math phobia," just as it has been argued that the very structure of the discipline has a masculine bias. This is a huge and complicated issue, and only its surface can be skimmed here. The fact is that through the age of thirteen, girls do as well as boys in mathematics. This is true not just for those with average scores, but among those at the highest levels as well. However, by age seventeen, when most seniors take the SAT, the girls have fallen behind. Yet by some indices, the gap has been closing. From 1978 to 1999, for example, nationwide tests of seventeen-year-olds found the girls rising from 35.4 percent of the highest scorers to 41.2 percent. However, during that period, the disparity in the sexes' SAT scores closed by a barely visible 1.5 percent.

Although we don't know if it is an actual fear of mathematics that girls and young women develop between thirteen and seventeen, something is clearly happening. Even among those who get good grades in the subject, not nearly as many girls as boys feel they are doing well. In one survey of high-performing students, only 38.9 percent of the girls said they thought their mathematical skills put them in the top 5 percent, whereas 57.1 percent of the boys placed themselves there. Also, 27.8 percent of the girls said they were "extremely anxious" about taking the SAT, compared with only 10.8 percent of the boys. As it turns out, feelings like these have consequences. Self-confidence works to your advantage more when faced with mathematics problems than on tests in other subjects, as will be seen.

During the past decade, the SAT has conducted successive studies, hoping to discover why boys answer more of its questions correctly. Rather than looking at everyone taking the test, they decided to focus on those who did best, choosing the 17.6 percent of the boys and 9.8 percent of the girls who scored at least 650 on the mathematics part. Their hypothesis was that here were girls who might have done better; so what kept them from doing so?

What emerged first was that the girls and boys did equally well on the introductory and intermediate questions, which was expected since they all scored over 650. The harder items at the end of the test were where the boys pulled ahead. However, the girls had taken essentially the same range of high school courses, they should have been ready for problems that called for a higher level of skills. What happened had less to do with their knowledge of the subject than with extrinsic factors.

Given the SAT's time constraints, questions must be addressed quickly, followed by a swift stab at a solution. Since, as was found, the boys had more confidence in their mathematical skills, they were, the SAT found, more willing to use "deductive, gestalt-type strategies that enable them to see the solution without actually working out the problem." In contrast, the girls were more cautious, relying "substantially more on algorithms taught in class and procedures outlined by the teacher."

Let's see how these sex differences show up on the tests. The table on the next page shows two kinds of questions, one where boys usually do better than girls, and another where girls tend to surpass boys. The first is actually a trick question. This is because to obtain the correct answer, the student would have to construct an involved algebraic equation, and there is no way that can be done in the allotted time. So girls are likely to leave this question blank and move on to the next one. Boys are more willing to size up the gist of the question and then gauge which might be the best answer. And frequently they get it right.

But taking shortcuts doesn't work well with the second kind of question. Boys often settle for a quick look at the size of the rectangles, where the one that seems the largest actually isn't. The girls read the

MEN'S MATH AND WOMEN'S MATH?

An SAT Question Where Men Outperform Women

A blend of coffee is made by mixing Colombian coffee at $8 a pound with espresso coffee at $3 a pound. If the blend costs $5 a pound, how many pounds of the Colombian coffee are needed to make 50 pounds of the blend?

(a) 20   (b) 25   (c) 30   (d) 35   (e) 40

An SAT Question Where Women Outperform Men

In the drawings below, each unit on the X-axis represents two inches and each on the Y-axis represents one inch. Which of the five rectangles has the greatest perimeter?

(a) A   (b) B   (c) C   (d) D   (e) E

Answers: (a) 20 Pounds & (b) Rectangle B

instructions more carefully, and keep in mind that one side of each box is really twice what it appears.

So two mathematical approaches are tested. One favors harelike boys, who race through all the questions; the other suits the more feminine tortoises, who tackle fewer questions but give them the attention they deserve. As presently designed, the SAT format gives boys the advantage, since it rewards a willingness to guess. Were there fewer problems, and more time to reflect on them, there seems little doubt that the girls—like tortoises—would do much better in the end. After all, this is supposed to be a test of reasoning ability, not a hundred-yard dash.

Questions are also designed so that good students of both sexes immediately see that three of the five possible answers are obviously wrong. The trick is to decide between the two remaining possibilities, and there the choice is usually quite close. Faced with this dilemma, it is always best to guess. The reason is in fact mathematical. Guessing doesn't help if you are completely ignorant, as if the test were in a language you didn't know. In that case, you would have only a 20 percent likelihood of picking the correct answer, and those odds are not worth chancing. But if you know that three of the five are wrong, a guess between the last two gives you a 50 percent chance of being right. (This is standard advice in coaching courses.) Whether it's bravado or intuition or a merited confidence, boys are willing to gamble, and often enough it turns out that they win. More often, girls skip the hardest questions, even though they realize that leaving an answer blank will pull down their score.

Thus the girls are almost three times as likely to bypass questions. For example, one item in the SAT study was skipped by 15.1 percent of the girls, but only 0.9 percent of the boys. On another, 17.3 percent of the women omitted it, compared with 0.8 percent of the boys. Had more of the girls the assurance to guess on these and other questions, more of their scores would have approached or matched the boys'. So at issue is how well the SAT measures mathematical ability, and how much its scores reward a knack for estimating answers, plus a willingness to gamble and to guess on this high-pressure 90-minute half of the test.

A way to resolve these disparities would be to change the format.

One possibility would be to allow students to take the test home over a weekend. There they could design their own schedule, including taking time off to return to questions to review and perhaps revise their answers. We'll assume they will abide by an honor code, and not seek outside assistance. (Are we so cynical as to feel that this wouldn't work?) Without a clock ticking, and with time for reflection, we would gain a better idea of how the sexes compare in this mysterious subject that we make our young people study and which most adults have long forgotten.

Whether more women will begin matching men in mathematics will become known fairly soon, as current trends are moving that way. In 1970, women comprised 37.4 percent of the undergraduate majors in mathematics, and by 2000 their share was 47.6 percent, or close to half. That men now dominate the heights of the discipline is a statistical fact. Among the students who in 2000 scored over 750, a close to perfect score, men were well ahead of women, by 17,152 to 7,422. But that's not the only way to look at these figures. Another fact is that those 7,422 young women had better scores than 97.1 percent of the boys who took the test that year. Since there are already that many women with a talent for the subject, there may well be considerably more waiting to be discovered and nurtured. At the least, we should take a closer look at those 7,422 to find out how they gained and use their skills, the settings where they were developed, along with the perspectives they bring to the subject and their feelings about themselves. With that as a start, we would have a better idea about whether mastery of mathematics requires a male gene.

Perhaps the most striking statistic in this chapter was that men are receiving only 42.8 percent of bachelor's degrees, so for every 100 women awarded diplomas, only 75 men are alongside them in the procession. This sexual mismatch means more than a lot of students won't be able to find a date. As the current cohort of women graduate into the larger society, they will also also find a shortfall of their male cultural peers. Examples of this and other asymmetries will recur in the next several chapters.

6

The Double Standard:
How Much Has Really Changed?

At first reading, the phrase in this chapter's title may seem old-fashioned and out-of-date. It evokes images of bachelors being sexually initiated, while virginal young women were made to stay at home. Or it recalls all the places where men could go freely, while unescorted women were not admitted or made to feel ill at ease.

Surely, the double standard has all but disappeared, or at least it is a shadow of its former self. After all, how many places can we cite that are still off-limits for women, and how many activities are there in which they cannot partake? Hardly more than a handful, and each year the number declines. Today, the country brims with independent, confident women, who refuse to tolerate bias or exclusion. All this may be true, as has been discussed throughout this book. Yet it is important to examine to what exent a double standard still exists, the forms it currently takes, and what may be its lingering effects.

Let's grant that disparate rules for the sexes are rarely specified in laws and policies. But many unspoken attitudes and assumptions remain in people's minds. And these retain a power to limit the options open to women; indeed, they degrade their human standing. How can ideas so outmoded and unfair remain so viable? One reason, as will be seen, is that the men who profit from the double standard have been adept at redrawing the boundaries of what they deem to be permissible conduct for women. After all, a society in 2003 cannot be expected to accept conventions common in 1903 or 1953.

Any woman can cite examples of how the double standard works, and they are generally showcases of disparate treatment. Some are literally built in bricks and mortar, as with theaters' rest-room facilities. Plus persisting instances where women face unwanted overtures, something few men can truthfully say has beleaguered them. Or take two colleagues who wish to appear attractive at work: which one will end up spending more time, money, and worry about making suitable choices? All told, little things—perhaps they're not so little—add up. Even today, some women who are traveling by themselves will have dinner sent up to their hotel room, rather than go to a restaurant alone. Very simply, they aren't entirely sure they would feel comfortable there, a worry men on their own would never have. In fact, they may first drop by the cocktail lounge and banter with other guys they find there.

Rather than attempt an exhaustive list of how the double standard persists, this chapter will focus on uneven responses to sexual liberation, as well as the unequal images of aging and opportunities for later mating.

JUST WORDS?

Words can hurt and humiliate, and many aim to do just that. The English language has a list of idioms, all created to injure women. The issue is not how these terms arose, but why they manage to persist. First are the hardy perennials: *slut, tramp, whore*. Or less crude, but serving a similar purpose: *loose, easy, available*. (The last assumed of women who walk into a cocktail lounge alone, as if ready for an overture.) In other contexts, there is *nymphomania*, a diagnosis only assigned to women, with no parallel term for men. This also holds for *promiscuous*, which is rarely affixed to men who aren't choosy about their partners or have had a multitude of them.

These words are meant to be weapons, held in reserve to keep women on edge. While not quite verbalized variants of rape, their aim is to warn women that they may be devalued, not just sexually, but by downgrading their status and impugning their character. In no way are men made vulnerable to the same degree. Indeed, the language has not a comparable set of words that can wreak the same damage on men.

Call a man a *stud,* a *Don Juan,* a *womanizer,* and he will preen. He will take them as testimony to his seductive skill, his charm, his ability to make women melt. If you call him a *satyr,* a *lecher,* or a *libertine,* he will ask what century you are living in. Doubtless there are psychiatric rubrics for men who seek to set sexual records. Yet whatever the labels, they lack the poignancy of *nymphomaniac.* True, there are some accusatory terms; but they put a precise burden on whoever levels the charge. Thus if you call him a *gigolo,* you had better have evidence that the woman he squires always picks up the tab. To make it stick that he is a *rapist,* charges serious enough for a prosecution must be leveled against him.

NUMBERS: HERS AND HIS

In the past, a bride was expected to be virginal, while the groom was presumed to be a man of experience. Nor was there concern about his partners: they could be from the lower classes, who were readily exploited; or older women initiating younger lovers; and, of course, prostitutes. A young woman's virginity was a social and moral asset; and an economic one if she wished to raise her status. Losing it would cause her value to diminish. Hence the warnings implicit in allusions to women said to have a *"past."*

There was one exception allowed. Instead of being virginal, a woman could be pregnant when she took her vows. Even in the 1950s, almost one bride in ten had a child on the way. (The real figure was probably higher, fudged by family doctors willing to register "a seven-month birth.") And with abortion not readily available, more young men were willing to "do the right thing," or did so under pressure. In this respect, the double standard in those days had a double edge. A young man who, as was said, deflowered a woman of his class was also made to pay a price. After all, an early, perhaps unwelcome, marriage, meant he had to relinquish his bachelor's freedom. However, as was noted earlier, most of those unions endured despite their inauspicious origins.

Aside from those who are especially religious, these days no one asks women to refrain from having premarital sex. Even so, the double standard doesn't give up easily, and persists by adapting to changed conditions. Girls and women contemplating premarital sex no longer hear it is absolutely out of the question. Rather, our more tolerant age advises them it is best not to have "too many" different partners. Thus while sex may be a part of a woman's life, she knows she must not appear to be too experienced in this area. Indeed, this is the current version of being a woman with a "past." Thus having had "too many" partners prior to marriage devalues her in much the same way that losing virginity did earlier. But *how many* partners may she have before *too many* weighs in? Here the current double standard is more insidious, if only because the answer is so subjective and dependent upon each person's circmustances. After all, today's women are getting married when they are older, and thus have more years of being single, including between and after marriages.

The numbers underscore this point: 38.9 percent of young women in their mid- to late twenties haven't yet married, and another 9.3 percent have but are now divorced or separated. A record high of 21.9 percent of women ages 30 to 34 are still unmarried, while another 12.5 percent were once wed but no longer are. But does this mean that women may indulge as freely as men? Certainly not. The label *"promiscuous"* is not yet moribund, and even some worldly women may worry whether they are crossing an unspecified line.

At the time this book was being written, there was an astute television program called "Sex and the City," about the lives amd loves and anxieties of single women in their mid-thirties. All four of the main characters were free spirits, fumbling in a mismatched arena of women and men. Yet in one scene, one is heard warning a friend that her sex life was heading "into the double digits." Even these urban sophisticates seem to agree that there can be "too many."

Liberal and open-minded men will often find themselves curious about the *pasts* of women whom they view as possible partners for a serious relationship. The man may wonder: would I be just another of *many* men with whom she's been intimate, including some who raise suspicions that she's not very selective? This isn't so far from the obsession with *virginity* common in earlier eras. And if the couple begins to get serious, he may start thinking about asking her the *"how many"* question. Well, yes, they may exchange anecdotes about former marriages or previous relationships. But he really wants to know *The*

Number. So much so, that he may actually ask for it. He may be vaguely aware of figures like those in the table on the next page, which are derived from a Department of Health and Human Services survey, and he wants to know in which category she falls. Might she, for example, be among the 20.5 percent who admit to having had at least ten partners? While modern men don't expect women to be virginal, they are not wholly unlike their grandfathers in wondering about a woman's "past." True, women also show a kindred curiosity about men they meet. But their concern is more about the likelihood of his future fidelity.

TRUTH AND LIES

Since the days of Alfred Kinsey, countless studies have asked people to reveal what they do in bed and other places. An ongoing problem is whether what they say is truthful. This became evident when the results of the 1994 nationwide study called *The Social Organization of Sexuality* were analyzed. Not surprisingly, one question asked how many different partners each respondent had had. (They were only asked about heterosexual sex.) The responses by the women in the sample gave them an average of 3.5 different men; while the men, by their accounts, averaged 12.7 women. That the men's figure was three to four times higher testifies to the greater opportunities available to them, which is part of the double standard. But it isn't easy to see how the numbers can coexist. For the men to average this many partners, there had to be some very active women who help them rack up their scores. (The interviewers intimated to the men that they should not count episodes with prostitutes.) However, only 2.9 percent of the women mentioned having twenty or more partners. This means that each of those women would have had to service several hundred men, and that doesn't seem very likely. So we're back to the issue of how candid people really are when discussing their sexual pasts.

All indications are that men are inclined to exaggerate their sexual success, even to interviewers they do not know and will never see again. It's almost as if they want their prowess recorded in some kind of archive, even if it's just a collection of statistics. Of course, mixing wishful thinking with the facts isn't an unusual occurrence. (Many people who haven't voted or donated blood tell pollsters that they have.) Women, on the other hand, tend to understate their sexual experience even when questioned by researchers of their own sex.

The Department of Health and Human Services decided to test this suspicion, when it was collecting figures for the table on this page. There, as can be seen, 9.0 percent of single women aged 25 to 29 said they had sex with four or more men in the past year. What should now be added is that for this question, they were asked to write out their answer anonymously, seal it in a blank envelope, and deposit it in a box in another room when the interview was over. In fact, this was one of a pair of surveys. In the second, a comparable group of women were also queried about their sex lives, however this time they were asked to answer aloud to a woman interviewer. In those cases, it was found, only 2.9 percent admitted to having four or more partners, in contrast to the 9.0 percent who replied anonymously.

HOW MANY SEXUAL PARTNERS?

All Women Age 35–39 Until Now		Single Women Age 25–29 Past Year Only
1.8%	None	17.3%
24.3%	1	50.0%
11.7%	2	18.3%
9.4%	3	5.4%
8.5%	4/4+	9.0%
9.3%	5	100.0%
14.5%	6–9	
20.5%	10+	
100.0%		

In one sense, the double standard has apparently eroded. What might be called the sexual experience gap has narrowed, and may no longer exist at all. (Why men still exaggerate will be discussed in the next chapter.) Where the differential persists is that while women are feeling freer to explore their sexuality, they may feel it prudent to be more reticent about the extent of their experience. But why such concern when they are with interviewers they haven't seen before and won't be seeing again? Here too they may be concerned that this information about themselves is being recorded somewhere. Or it could be that they regret some of their encounters, and giving a lower number is one way of erasing them. This too reflects the double standard, since men are less likely to have rueful feelings about their part in such occasions.

DIFFERENTIAL DEPRECIATION

For most of us, we think of *depreciation* in terms of physical objects like automobiles. Some cars have high resale values and preserve their worth for longer periods. This is usually because they use higher-grade materials and are built with greater care, and keep performing well over many years. But valuations can also have a less rational side, as when someone doesn't want to be seen owning a car that looks too old. The auto industry is fully aware of this concern, and capitalizes on it by introducing new models each year, so everyone can know how old your car is.

The ways valuations are placed on women do not differ greatly from those for cars or pickup trucks. We've all heard the tired joke about men turning in their current wives for newer models. This is yet another application of the double standard, which posits that women will depreciate at a faster rate than men. Of course, this is not actually decreed, but owes its force to public perception of two sexes. While a man and a woman may both have been fifty years on this earth, more often than not the woman is perceived as being *older,* and hence of lesser worth. (Nor does turning fat and bald necessarily downgrade a man's value.)

There is no need to detail the multibillion-dollar industry devoted to forestalling depreciation. The products range from lotions and

WHO GETS ANOTHER CHANCE?

Ages of Men and Women Who Remarry

Brides	Own Age	Grooms
50.0%	Under 35	37.3%
31.3%	35–44	33.7%
18.7%	Over 44	29.0%
100.0%		100.0%

Men and Women Aged 45–54 Who Remarry:
How Old Are Their New Mates?

Brides	Age of Spouse	Grooms
1.8%	Under 30	7.9%
3.5%	30–34	12.4%
19.9%	35–44	46.2%
45.3%	45–54	30.0%
29.5%	Over 54	3.5%
100.0%		100.0%

creams to tailored garments and exercise equipment. Services run an equally wide gamut, from hair coloring to cosmetic surgery. Whether, or to what extent, these contrivances succeed, is another issue. But women continue to be the primary purchasers of these products. And hope must persist, as evidenced by the enormous amounts of money spent each year for these goods and services. True, increasing numbers of men are turning to hair treatments, eye adjustments, and wrinkle removal. While some are just plain vain or fearful about their careers, others are divorced men in their fifties hoping to attract a trophy second mate.

The 2000 Census counted 2,479,000 women between the ages of 40 and 44 who had been married but no longer were. But it located only 1,998,000 formerly married men of that age. As equal numbers of men and women are parties to divorces, and being widowed at this age is fairly rare, why are there 481,000 more women in this group? In fact, we know the answer: men that age have a greater chance to remarry, and they take advantage of that opportunity.

When men remarry, it is generally to younger women. At first weddings, as has been noted, the average groom is less than two years older than his bride. But when he sets about choosing a second mate, he looks for a wider gap. As it turns out, he will not find a shortage of willing candidates. Few women are biased against older men, so long as they aren't doddering. The table on the previous page shows that among the men and women who remarry, 29.0 percent of the grooms are older than 44, against 18.7 percent of the brides. Or note the range of choices for remarrying men aged 45 to 54. Two thirds of them find brides ten years their junior, and one-fifth get a willing partner twenty years younger.

Women who show ambition are less likely to marry or stay in that state. (But wasn't that the theme of so many Joan Crawford and Rosalind Russell movies?) The table on the next page focuses on individuals who earned over $100,000 in 2000. The men made up the top 15.1 percent of workers their age, while the women represented the top 3.4 percent. So this is a selective group of women, who are committed to careers and have done well in them. And the table shows that women at this level are over twice as likely to have never been married and almost four times as apt to have been in marriages that didn't last. These findings provide precise numbers for what we already know: fewer men find it difficult to combine a marriage with professional demands. The situations women face are less clear-cut.

While this is not quite a chicken-and-egg problem, there are several possible scenarios. One is that women who find they are on their own, and thus must support themselves, will work to improve their financial status. We all know many women who are in such situations, and their numbers will grow in the years ahead. But in another context, it could be proposed that women who have the kinds of attributes that bring them high earnings find it harder to locate mates they regard as suitable, or to keep a marriage going when they do. Insofar as the paucity of pairings comprises a problem, it arises partly because accomplished women are setting standards for men that not enough of them seem able to meet. But it in part rests with men, who don't want the demands that often come with a woman who has created a life of her own. That fewer women harbor this worry about potential mates reveals not only a double standard, but that some women are helping to perpetuate it.

In the past, husbands left their wives for chorus girls or manicurists, at least in the Hollywood depictions. Now they are more inclined to be drawn to younger women in their own or similar professions. Let's look in on a holiday party at a law firm, where members have been invited to bring their spouses. Almost all the senior partners come with their original wives, who are close to their own age. Also in attendance are the young associates of the firm, half of whom are now likely to be women, many of them unmarried.

Now witness what happens as the evening proceeds. After early civilities, where the husbands and wives stand next to each other, separate circles begin forming. In one group will be the lawyers, engaging in legal chat. In another are the partners' wives, exchanging social amenities. But look again where the lawyers are clustered. Among them will be the women members of the firm, if not at the center of the conversation, still ready to offer observations revealing their pro-

---

WHAT PRICE SUCCESS?

(Persons Earning Over $100,000)

Men	Marital Status	Women
84.6%	Currently Married	51.4%
8.4%	Formerly Married*	31.7%
7.0%	Never Married	16.9%
100.0%		100.0%

*And not currently remarried

---

fessional competence. The wives of the partners are quite aware of how their husbands are at ease with the younger women. This is how they interact at work, as well as at business dinners and on out-of-town travels. Surely, at least some of the wives may feel threatened.

WHAT WOMEN STILL FACE

The double standard owes its power to the resilience of ideas that become embedded over the years. Accepting what exists is always easier than contemplating change. It's not that people are inherently conservative, but rather that they're uncertain about what might replace the status quo. So even women who wish to remedy injustices that exist do not know what their lives would be like if changes were achieved. As has been stressed throughout this book, men now face competition from women, and the women are often winning. Accordingly, men already have an inkling of what a more egalitarian future may hold for them. Gloria Steinem once wrote that "if women's liberation wins, we all gain." By no means are all men sure they agree.

It has become a hallmark of our time that women, far more than men, must juggle the competing demands of work and family life. It is they, much more than men, who must figure out what persona to show at work, from what you wear to how you speak. Women with careers also have to be tactful with female friends and relatives who have taken more traditional paths, and who may be uneasy with others' recognition and success. This is seldom something men need to consider, nor do they have to face judgments about choices they make and the lives they create. Nor need they worry about whether they will find a mate who will love and accept them for the strong, smart, earnest individuals that they are.

As women have become more comfortable asserting themselves in the workplace and on the home front, it's not surprising that at least some men have found this change intimidating. Indeed, it calls into question ideas about what it means to be a man, which is the topic of the next chapter.

7

The Fragility of Masculinity

Being a man can mean many things, from the trivial to the titanic. A lot of it has to do with physical strength, as men are expected to protect women from danger, which is often in the form of other men. In our times, however, most men do not find themselves called on to ward off marauders. Indeed, growing numbers of women say they don't want or need this protection. While not all are studying karate or taking self-defense classes, a glance at gyms and running tracks shows they are matching men in these and other regimens. Indeed, in spheres calling for physical stamina and skill, more women than ever before are showing the kinds of strengths once seen as mainly masculine.

Much is said about how ours has become an information economy, where verbal dexterity is expected and the principal products are words and symbols and numbers. Today, most occupations require prolonged sitting, whether at desks or cubicles, or in a car or in the air. Insofar as sweat is exuded, it is mainly on the brow, due to stresses related to meetings or bosses or other concerns about careers. The great majority of American men now have indoor employment, usually in air-conditioned offices far from oil fields, forests, or factory floors. Is this really "men's work"?

To some, that phrase may have an antediluvian ring, connoting brawn over brains, and repetitive routines, not to mention grimy blue collars and coarse expletives. In fact, the kinds of work most men ordinarily did in the past could be difficult and dangerous. There are still such jobs, and they continue to be male preserves. According to the Bureau of Labor Statistics, most garage mechanics are still men

(98.5 percent); as are roofers (98.2 percent); firefighters (97.3 percent); airline pilots (96.5 percent); loggers (97.8 percent); and crane and tower operators (97.9 percent).

So how does a male establish his manhood, especially if the work he does can readily be done by women, and increasingly is? There are several recourses; some are obvious, while others can be subtle; some are all but universal, while others have specific settings. In the American Southwest, for example, men who have never sat in a saddle wear cowboy boots as if to affirm that they would be at home on a range. (President George W. Bush, who calls his Texas home a ranch, doesn't ride a horse.) Apparently enough men are still lured by the Marlboro advertisements, which invite them to join the cowhands out at the corral. Or witness the popularity of "sports utility vehicles." They are veritable tanks, which enable the driver to wrest the road from lesser creatures in conventional cars. And, as with the Marlboro man, the SUV easily induces fantasies of forsaking suburban roads for untamed canyons and arroyos. (True, some women drive these vehicles, but if you look on any highway, you'll see mainly men's hands on the wheels.)

As for owning guns, we are continually made aware of how important this is for the millions of men who do. Some confine themselves to rifles, which are used mainly for shooting ducks and deer. There are, of course, many reasons why men are drawn to hunting. But high on the list is to emulate what "real men" used to do: venturing in the wild to bring back sustenance for their women and children. Nor does it matter that venison rarely shows up on their family's dinner table. The point is that the man of the house is showing that he *could* be that basic provider were events to make it necessary.

Other men prefer handguns, whose principal purpose is to kill or disable people. Here the owners are affirming that they will protect their home or other premises from intruders intent on robbery or worse. It is irrelevant that most of the people who own guns live in regions where such intrusions are rare. (Though few actual trespassers are waylaid, all too often we hear of children slaying siblings or playmates with a parent's gun.) Needless to say, guns are also associated with the untamed West, when America's manhood was in its finest hour. Or when the doughty Minutemen pushed back the minions of an oppressive overlord. Sentiments like these are still with us today, in this more sedentary age, prompting men to insist on their right to bear and use weapons that affirm their potency. It is arguable how many women are impressed with men who want guns in a pickup truck or a bedside stand. A table appearing later in this chapter will show that women are considerably more likely to favor gun control laws, which also reflects their desire to have fewer firearms in private hands.

Another measure of manhood is to side with police officers, especially when they face charges of bias or brutality. After all, they are trained professionals; they can tell when someone is a probable perpetrator. A phrase often heard is that these public servants *"put their lives on the line every day."* Given this daily exposure to danger, they should be allowed to conclude that any hand moving toward a pocket may be reaching for a revolver. Should they hesitate about firing first if the outcome could be their lives?

In fact, far fewer police officers are slain by criminals than is commonly believed. In 2000, of the nation's 637,511 law enforcement officers, a total of 51 died in direct confrontations with felons. (Another 84 lost their lives in accidents, usually while driving.) In 2001, direct encounters led to 69 deaths, and another 71 died in the World Trade Center. However, the actual numbers are not the point. Again, the police serve as symbols of men who do man's work. So it is not coincidental that every television season features several programs depicting police valor on mean urban streets. Equally revealing is that most of the male viewers are encouched in suburban living rooms. One doesn't need a psychoanalytic degree to suspect that identifying with the police is indicative of a desire to absorb some of the power and prowess they are thought to have.

MARINES AND GREEN BERETS

The very term "hawk" has a masculine mien, which cannot easily be said of "dove." Those who give peace a high priority are seen as wimps or nerds or cowards, belonging in the company of women. (Try as they will to sound tough, Democrats never quite manage to pull it off.) Hollywood has always known how to attract men to the movies. From John Wayne to Clint Eastwood and Sylvester Stallone—note the intimation in the last name—men go to see their illusory selves on the screen. In the dark, they can imagine they are embodying courage, inner strength, and indifference to pain. If much of their day is spent staring at desktop screens, they can muse that they have what it takes to be out there with the Marines and Green Berets.

Hence their enthusiasm for formidable American arsenals, including billion-dollar submarines and bombers. The table on the next page shows that 71 percent of the men in a *Washington Post* poll support a costly missile defense, well ahead of 51 percent of the women. Nor should they be seen simply as favoring a shield against an external attack. It is much more than that. The system known as Star Wars fuses technology with an ideology. It expresses the conviction that the United States must remain a formidable military presence, as befits being the leading power in the world. Given the envy and enmity around the globe, in this view, we will always have enemies and must be prepared to stare them down. While few modern men know it, this is a legacy of Alexander Hamilton, who wrote, "I acknowledge my aversion to every project that is calculated to disarm the government of a single weapon which in any possible contingency might be usefully employed for the general defense and security." As befits a man of action, he gave his life defending his honor in a duel.

Nor is it a coincidence that the death penalty has become so pronounced an issue in our time. The United States is one of the few countries to retain this punishment, and the only one of those with which we like to compare ourselves. In 2001, there were 66 executions, with over 3,000 inmates awaiting that fate. Here, too, men are more likely than women to support capital punishment. As with favoring a militant foreign policy, such a stance attests to one's virility. Few men ever have a chance to confront a murderer and slay him at the scene, which is an ancient badge of manhood and the finale of many action movies. But short of that, they can at least imagine attending an execution and watching as the miscreant gasps his final breath.

THE FRAGILITY OF MASCULINITY

GAPS: POLITICS AND GENDER

Favor or Oppose Stricter Gun Control Laws?

	Men	Women
Favor	49%	71%
Oppose	51%	29%
	100%	100%

Support a Missile Defense System
That Could Cost as Much as $100 Billion?

	Men	Women
Favor	71%	51%
Oppose	29%	49%
	100%	100%

Should President Clinton Be Charged with Crimes
and Tried After He Leaves Office?

	Men	Women
Should Be	52%	42%
Should Not	48%	58%
	100%	100%

Washington Post polls, from August 2000 to January 2001.
Figures represent persons who expressed opinions.

113

PARADIGMS FOR POTENCY

Visualize someone who seems to embody the major attributes of masculinity. Make him a linebacker on a leading football team, who absorbs pain and punishment, giving his all without hogging the glory. Surely, this is the apotheosis of a man, and not a caricature. But then add another detail, a fact hardly anyone knows. For the past several years, he has been incapable of having an erection. Well, yes, he's still a man; or at least politeness makes us want to say so. Yet at least some may find themselves thinking that he has failed a primal test. (At the same time, they might be annoyed with themselves for entertaining such a thought.)

Femininity usually means having qualities that are conducive to attracting a man or successive men. From another vantage point it is tied to fertility: the ability to conceive and bear a child. If a woman is capable of conception, as most are, there is little she need do, other than take part in a coupling. There is no male term that is analogous to fertility, since all that is required is penetration and ejaculation, which can be completed in seconds. Even so, it doesn't always turn out to be so simple. In order for a conception to take place, a man must first have an erection, which cannot always be attained precisely when desired.

In the past, a man was deemed to be a man if he fathered a brood of children. And most passed that test, without anxiety or embarrassment, since siring a child didn't require special skills. So as the modern age evolved, a new paradigm for potency appeared. In the 1700s, the bar was raised, with the laurels now reserved for the lothario, the Casanova, the cavalier; in short, the man who had won the hearts of many women.* Some might be blessed with good looks and a fine physique. But what was really needed was a charismatic charm and an intuitive understanding of what women want and want to hear. Of

---

*A seducer named Lothario was featured in a 1703 play by Nicholas Rowe. Giovanni Casanova himself lived from 1725 to 1798. Mozart's *Don Giovanni* was first performed in 1787, while Byron's epic poem *Don Juan* appeared in installments from 1819 to 1824.

course, the aim here is to beguile them into bed. Manhood, thus measured, is not merely a matter of recording conquests. They must also satisfy qualitative criteria, with seductions gauged by moral and aesthetic norms. For example, the woman must have been a knowing participant, in no way coerced or cruelly deceived. Nor can she be unusually young or naive, plied with alcohol, or be emotionally vulnerable. By the same token, she cannot be too experienced, or too willing, since this manner of man is rated for his victories where others have failed.

How many men satisfy this model of manhood? Men who boast about their prowess are prone to hyperbole, if not outright prevarication. But the point is not how many men have matched the records of a Don Juan or John Kennedy or James Bond—two of whom happen to be fictional. Much more germane is that so many men dream and fantasize about enjoying an endless array of partners. These reveries move from visualizing a woman, to undressing her in his mind, and then imagining their tryst. Such flights of thought can happen thousands of times in a man's lifetime, and very likely do. On these occasions, the dreamer is becoming fully a man, a monarch of the forest, who can have his way with any female who strikes his fancy.* (More problematical is whether he wants these encounters to lead to pregnancies. While that would scatter his genes around his fantasized world, it could also bring on a lot of unwanted complications.)

NOW SHE DOES THE JUDGING

Recounting conquests is basically a man's game, with boasts often bolstered by beer, at places and occasions where women are understandably absent. By and large, these renderings center on what he did and how he did it, with little or nothing said about what the encounter

---

*Be warned, a bad joke is to follow; but it illustrates a point made in the text. On a balmy afternoon, two men are walking along Rodeo Drive in Beverly Hills. As an attractive woman passes, one man whispers to the other, "I've had her." His friend is impressed. Another really beautiful woman passes. "I've had her, too," the first man remarks. A little later, a woman who is utter perfection comes by. "I suppose you'll say that you've also had her," the friend jeers. "Sssh," the other says, *"I'm having her now."*

may have meant to his partner. But these bursts of bravado have been losing their veneer. One consequence of the sexual revolution of the 1960s is that women have different ideas about what their sex lives should be like. In addition, because they're getting married at later ages, there is more time to experience different partners, if they so choose. As a result, they now expect more from the men in their beds. This means that a man's potency is no longer certified by the cheers of his chums. Rather, to be validated as a man, he must demonstrate that he can satisfy women, emotionally and physically. The former has been discussed in other chapters, and will be alluded to again. On the physical side, we enter an area that is not always openly addressed. Impotence is usually viewed as an inability to attain an erection. Hence the huge sales of Viagra, which over seven million men were using a year after its introduction. That this many have tried it is evidence of the incidence of impotence, and of how anxious men are for a remedy.

It's a known fact that women typically take longer to become aroused and reach sexual climax. For this to occur in conventional intercourse, a man must be able to maintain his erection for at least several minutes or, indeed, considerably longer, so his partner can climax several times, yet another area where women surpass men. Insofar as this is what women would like, few men seem able to make this part of their anatomy retain its staying power. In most sexual studies, about three quarters of the men say they almost always achieve an orgasm, but less than 30 percent of the women report they do. The main reason why so many women don't is that most men succumb to what is called, usually in whispers, "premature ejaculation." And *premature* means just that: reaching a climax before he *should*. Which is to say that a real man should be able to delay himself until his partner is fully satisfied.

So a man's masculinity now depends on how his partner rates his performance. For years, she would assure him, *"It was just fine for me, dear."* However, men now find themselves wondering whether their mates are being truthful, since their manliness hangs in the balance. And might she just possibly be sharing her assessments with her girlfriends?

A WOMAN'S PRESIDENT?

Opinions about President William Jefferson Clinton reflected another division between the sexes. While hardly on the political left, he aroused the rancor of many conservatives. To them, he represented everything they didn't like about the 1960s, ranging from licentious indulgence to doubtful patriotism. In his 1996 reelection bid, only 43 percent of American men supported him, whereas 54 percent of women voters did, which was the largest gender gap in the history of presidential contests. Four years later, following his impeachment trial, a poll asked men and women whether Clinton should face further charges after leaving office. Their responses, also reproduced on the table on page 113, show that while a small majority of men wanted an indictment, women were quite emphatic in opposing that proposal.

Clinton was a man women were drawn to, in ways never seen before at so high a political level. I am not referring simply to his escapades with interns and others. Rather, he had a manner of speaking and listening to women that made them feel he cared about them. He may have been an unfaithful husband, a callous father, and not quite the model one wants in public office. Yet he still had a roguish allure that many women found attractive. Perhaps his scampish sexuality reminded them of an audacious boyfriend or brother. In their view, he was very much a man.

If this is how many women felt, at least some men, notably impeachment prosecutors like Kenneth Starr and Henry Hyde, may have wished to bring down a Casanova whose exploits they secretly envied. (This would help to explain all the prurient details recounted in their indictment.) If their attempt to humiliate Clinton drew little support from women, one reason may have been that they could see his enemies were driven by their own sexual insecurities.

A RACE FACTOR

In the United States, if not elsewhere, racial and sexual tensions intertwine. Imagine this scene, now not uncommon on a city street or a college campus. A well-built black man and an attractive white woman are strolling together. She gazes at him fondly. He returns her expression with self-assurance. How do white men react upon seeing this pair? As few will openly admit what is on their minds, we are left to speculate. Perhaps some will try to imagine *what* this pair does together, in particular what she does with and to him. Compounding the sexual insecurities that beset many men, white men harbor a primal fear that black men may surpass them in virility and performance. Not only that, there is an added apprehension: that white women may wonder whether sex with a black man would indeed be more satisfying. The issue, of course, is not whether these forebodings are true; rather it is that figments like these are in place and show few signs of going away.

In earlier times, white men responded to these fears with periodic lynchings, often preceded by castrations, to warn black men that they would do well to avert their eyes when white women were around. Today, the surrogate for lynching is imprisonment. As of this writing, almost a million black men languish in the nation's prisons, comprising more than half of the inmate population. To be sure, each one is there for having violated a law. Yet when the racial ratio rises that high, it makes sense to consider whether black men are also being locked in cages to suppress a sexual threat.

Here is another scene, also observed in cities and college settings: another couple is walking together, but this time the young man is white and the young woman is Chinese-American. These pairings are seen enough—including in wedding announcements—to need some explanation. To start, we can assume that the young men, in choosing as they have, find women of Asiatic ancestry attractive and congenial. But something more subtle is involved. Informal conversations with the men reveal that they also find them less assertive than women of their own race. Needless to say, the Asian women are intelligent and accomplished, and are fully aware of how the world works. Indeed, as was noted in chapter 5, they now outnumber Asian men at college. They are neither geishas nor groupies, nor do they in any way feel they are an inferior sex. At the same time, their upbringing has stressed the importance of being tactful, which is how men wish to be treated, even as they are quick to proclaim that they want women to be independent in mind and spirit. But in more confidential moments, more than a few will say that women of their own race often put them on the defensive, which is a burden that becomes wearying.

While there are no statistics on campus dating, we have information on what may happen later on. Census figures for 2000 on white-Asian marriages showed that the husband was white and the wife was Asian in 74.4 percent of these couples. A similar imbalance was found in black-white unions, where 77.2 percent of them had a black husband and a white wife. So while white women are drawn more to black than Asian men, white men tend to choose Asian women over black women.

MUSCLING IN

For the longest time, sports and athletics have been men's domains. More than that, they have been major arenas where men have proved themselves, with those who excel becoming models for their sex. Of course, many women played tennis, and schools had girls' field hockey teams. But all in all, few women went in for physical activity in more than a marginal way. Indeed, if you walked by a high school on an autumn afternoon, you would see boys at football scrimmage, while girls dutifully watched them on the sidelines or practiced their cheerleading routines.

All this has changed, and radically, in the last thirty years. Much of the credit must go to Title IX of the Education Act Amendments of 1972, which has been interpreted as requiring that colleges' athletic spending for facilities and scholarships must be allocated to men and women according to their numbers on a campus. Since 1972, women's intercollegiate teams have more than doubled, and the students on them have increased fivefold, from 30,000 to 157,000. But since the athletic budgets at most schools tend to be finite, the arrival of women has had its costs. Some of the trade-offs are reported in a 2001 General Accounting Office study, which charted changes between 1981 and 1998.

During those seventeen years, the number of women's teams rose by 3,784, while men's grew by only 36. As a result, across the country, there are now actually more women's teams. Among the most graphic was the increase in women's soccer squads, from 80 to 926. On the other side of the ledger, 56 colleges dropped men's gymnastics, 171 discontinued wrestling, and 45 no longer have men's track. UCLA dropped men's swimming, Providence College ended baseball, and Boston University closed out its football team. Most have also capped the number of men who can play, so their coaches must make do with smaller squads.*

Intercollegiate sports for either sex can be expensive. The costs of air tickets and hotel rooms can add up. In the fall of 2000, for exam-

---

THE NEW YORK MARATHON: WOMEN WHO RUN (AND WIN)

	1980	1990	2002
Runners	12,512	23,774	31,824
Men	87.0%	84.4%	68.0%
Women	13.0%	15.6%	32.0%
Total	100.0%	100.0%	100.0%

The First 100 Finishers

Winners	1980	1990	2002
Men	99	95	84
Women	1	5	16
	100	100	100

---

*If fact, the real reason why some men's teams are dropped has not been the advent of women's lacrosse or water polo. Rather, it is that by far the largest slice of the men's athletic budget goes to football. Squads even at smaller schools may average more than ninety players, with many on the field for only a few minutes. If colleges could make do with, say, sixty players, as professional football does, then teams like wrestling and gymnastics would not have to be cut.

ple, Stanford's women's volleyball team had thirteen games away, almost one every week, including trips to Arizona and Utah. The following spring, Stanford's women's softball players journeyed as far afield as Oklahoma, Florida, and Georgia. Two hundred schools now have women's lacrosse teams, which average 22 players per squad. Each year, the number of women who receive athletic scholarships, or admissions preference for playing a sport, approaches that for men.

For their part, women take their sports seriously. Nor is this only true among college athletes. The National Center for Health Statistics found that among young people aged 18 to 24, fewer women than men were overweight, by a margin of 28 percent. And in the 30 to 44 age range, women were 25 percent more likely than men to engage in "regular vigorous activity." Women hold the records in long-distance swimming, having beaten men both in the 22-mile race from Long Beach to Catalina Island and the 26 miles around Manhattan Island.

Of course, due to differences in physiology, the top-ranked men's team in any sport will defeat the leading women's team. Similarly, in golf and tennis, men stars will beat the best women. So it would be useful to look at a sport where the sexes take part together, even when times or scores are recorded separately. A good case is the New York City Marathon, where applicants are given places on merit. The figures in the table on the previous page show that from 1980 to 2002, the number of women entrants increased sixfold, while the number of men hardly doubled. This means that fewer new men are applying, while more women are. Put another way, the pool of men who wish to run the race isn't changing, while that of women clearly is.

But at least equally striking is that each year, more women are among the first 100 to finish, a super-elite group that in 2002 included only one third of one percent of all who completed the race. That year, there were sixteen women in the first 100 to cross the tape, which meant they came in ahead of 99.6 percent of the men in the race. While men will always prevail when it comes to lifting weights, on a terrain that is equally demanding to both sexes—and a marathon is surely that—more women are passing and surpassing thousands of men each year.

A NEW COMPETITION

It remains to be seen whether *manhood* can survive continuing victories by women, whether in long-distance racing or admission to selective colleges. In earlier times, few men had to confess that they had lost to a woman in some crucial competition. After all, women weren't applying to medical school, but settled for becoming nurses. Nor were there more than a handful of cases where men failed to receive judgeships, university presidencies, or cabinet positions, due to decisions to appoint a woman. That of course has changed. Losing is one thing; even trial attorneys have their share of defeats. But for men to lose out to women is new and different. We will soon see—if we are not already—how far the self-assurance associated with manliness can survive when each year sees more appointments and promotions going to the other sex.

8

The Ultimate Assault:
Why Rape Persists

In all ages, including our own, some men take the notion of masculinity to an extreme, and use their strength or threatening weapons to rape or assault women. Of course, not all men rape. Indeed, most men never will, even when in situations where they would not be caught or censured. But others do succumb when occasions arise. In wartime, another way to humiliate an enemy is by violating their women. More common are the offenses that pass for rites of manhood along fraternity row. But even here lines become shadowy: does plying a freshman woman with spiked punch turn the sex that follows into rape?

WHEN, WHERE, HOW OFTEN?

Not surprisingly, it isn't easy to obtain reliable figures on the frequency of rape. For one thing, people can disagree about whether what happened was really rape or perhaps something else. For example, does the woman have to show she fought back, or be bruised and battered, or could force take other forms? There may also be questions about the accuracy of memory, as well as whether victims are prone to fabrications or fantasies or vindictiveness. When surveys are taken, there is the possibility that interviewers may prompt certain responses or encourage overstatements. Rape is a serious matter, with political overtones.

Gathering information on it is not like asking about preferences in breakfast cereals.

As it happens, three agencies within the Department of Justice publish separate sets of figures on rape and other sexual crimes. Best known is the Federal Bureau of Investigation, which gathers information from state and local police forces throughout the country. In 2000, those agencies received 90,186 reports of rape, mainly from the victims. The same departments also disclosed that 46.9 percent of the cases were "cleared," signifying an arrest or conviction, or that the charges were dropped or withdrawn. But this percentage also suggests that culprits weren't found for over half the incidents. As will be seen, most victims concede they knew the perpetrator, and could identify him and his whereabouts. But relatively few of these acquaintance rapes are reported. So the police hear mostly about incidents involving total strangers, who are much harder to locate and arrest.

Another arm of the Justice Department, its Bureau of Justice Statistics, conducts an annual "victimization" survey, which asks a nationwide sample of households if their members experienced any crimes during the last year. Extrapolating from those responses, it estimated that 92,000 women were raped in 2000, which is about the same as the FBI figure, and an additional 55,000 women said they fended off unsuccessful attempts. The study also uncovered 114,000 *sexual assaults* against women, which were distinguished from the completed and deflected rapes. These additional crimes are not very helpfully defined as "a wide range of victimizations involving attacks in which unwanted sexual contact occurs between the victim and the offender." Making it even less useful, this assault category also conflates offenses against both adults and juveniles. For all 261,000 of the sexual crimes, added together, we are told:

- 47.9 percent were reported to law enforcement authorities.
- 2.8 percent of the assailants had a gun, 3.6 percent had a knife, and in 93.6 percent no weapon was used or present.
- 19.1 percent of the assailants were a current or former spouse or a boyfriend; 2.0 percent were other relatives, including stepfathers; 43.5 percent were acquaintances or friends; and 35.4 percent were strangers.

Yet another study, published by the National Institute of Justice in 1998, conducted face-to-face interviews with the women in its sample. From those sessions, it extrapolated that there had been 876,000 rapes and sexual assaults the previous year. But this figure included all unwanted advances, including those by a husband or an intimate partner. Indeed, the study specifically asked for recollections of rapes within marriage or by boyfriends.

The Bureau of Justice Statistics also collates information on victims of sexual crimes. The figures, which are summarized in the table on the next page, were derived from the court records of offenders who were convicted in 1995. Here, too, the majority of victims were relatives or known to their assailants. The saddest statistics are that 15.2 percent of rape victims and 44.7 percent who suffer sexual assaults were under the age of thirteen.

How many women have been victims? As has been indicated, a lot depends on definitions. A study of 4,163 Massachusetts high school students found 9.1 percent saying they had been sexually abused by someone they had been dating. In another study, of 3,187 college women, 15.0 percent said they had already been raped one or more times. Of these, four out of five added that they knew the man, and half had been in a dating relationship with him. Yet another analysis, published by the National Institute of Justice in 2000, examined the experience of 4,446 college women. In this sample, 1.8 percent said they had been raped during the previous year, while another 1.3 percent had thwarted attempted rapes, a category including "verbal threats." At least as striking was that 10.1 percent said they had been raped, and 10.9 percent had suffered attempts, prior to the year about which they were being questioned.

As for men, it would be of interest to know how many have been assailants, or made attempts, or will do so sometime before they die. The accurate answer is that no one knows, nor will we ever know for sure. Needless to say, we have no shortage of studies in which men are asked about their sexual experiences.

But hardly any inquire about conduct so egregious as to be felonious. In one survey, 60 percent of a sample of college men said that they had used force at least once to get their way with women. If this group is representative of all members of their sex, it means the

VICTIMS OF SEXUAL CRIMES

	Forcible Rape	Other Sexual Assaults
Median Age	22 years	13 years
Under 13	15.2%	44.7%
13 to 17	21.8%	33.0%
18 to 24	25.1%	9.4%
25 to 34	25.4%	7.7%
Over 34	12.5%	5.2%
	100.0%	100.0%
Relation to Offender		
Child or Stepchild	14.0%	25.9%
Wife or Former Wife	1.5%	1.4%
Other Relative	5.1%	11.2%
Girlfriend	8.8%	5.4%
Casual Acquaintance	40.8%	41.2%
Stranger	29.8%	14.9%
	100.0%	100.0%

The men in prison for assaults other than rape had been convicted of acts with children (25%); statutory rape (3%); forcible sodomy (5%); and molestation, fondling, and similar offenses (67%). Of the victims, 85% were girls or women and 15% were boys or men.

Information about victims derived from the court records of offenders convicted in 1995.

country has more than 50 million rapists in its midst, or at least that many men willing to use some form of coercion to get the sex they want. Or the figure may be higher, as some men have not yet acted, but may later on. Since the survey didn't cover men who weren't in college, the numbers could be even greater, as arrest records show that men with less education are more often indicted for sex crimes. This class aspect will be considered later.

FROM LABORATORY TO LIFE

Many men fantasize about rape, usually with themselves as the perpetrators. Interestingly, a common feature of these imagined scenes is that the woman ends up confessing she enjoyed it, and even finds herself attracted to the man who subdued her. Such reveries do more than swell the egos of the men who create them. They also solidify the view that, despite women's objections, they unconsciously want to be raped.

Howard Barbaree, a Canadian psychologist, has conducted some imaginative experiments showing the settings and circumstances that can lead men to rape. True, these are laboratory exercises, removed from the real world. But let's suspend doubt for a moment and see what he discovered.

Dr. Barbaree first fitted a group of men with a device called a *penile plethysmograph,* which gauged their sexual arousal by calibrating how much blood flowed to their genitals. They were then shown two types of pornographic movies, both of which had detailed depictions of sexual acts. In the first kind, the sex was portrayed as consensual, where the women were seen enjoying the encounters. The device reported that most of the men were stimulated by this film, which might be expected. They were then shown the second feature, which purported to depict rapes, with violence enacted in vivid detail, and where the women reacted with panic and pain. The devices showed little or no sexual arousal while the men were watching these scenes. So this part of the experiment validated a widely held view: that forced sex is not a turn-on for most men. But this was only Act I of the test.

During a break in the study, the men were taken to separate rooms, where they were asked to pedal a stationary bicycle as fast as they could, on which their mileage would be recorded. (They were told it had to do with genital arousal.) When each man had finished, a young woman walked in and looked at the distance he had gone. *"Is this the best you could do?"* she sneered, and then added, *"The women we've been testing are doing a lot better than you have."* She then stalked out, without waiting for a reply.

Another member of the research staff then ushered the men in to see a new pair of movies, much like those they had seen before. But this time, the devices found that the films that portrayed violent rapes were now arousing them sexually, as much as or even more than the consensual ones had earlier. They were especially stirred when the story lines intimated that the women playing the victims deserved the maulings they were getting. Might they have been recalling that woman who had mocked their masculinity several minutes earlier?

Of course, studies in a laboratory are removed from real life. Still, Professor Barbaree started with a physiological reality. A man's penis engorges much less because of conscious commands than in response to stirrings outside his control. The fact that the plethysmograph registered arousal on the second viewing of violent sex, after the men had been ridiculed by a woman, conveyed what interviews never could. That is, even if the men said they were disgusted by the depicted rapes, their penises were telling a different story. There is still the question of whether arousal connotes approval of the assaults, not to mention identifying with the rapist. At the least, they were excited by what they saw, whereas that hadn't happened during the earlier viewing. That fact is worth pondering.

IN MEN'S GENES?

Why does rape persist? Despite reams of research directed to this question, the answer remains elusive. Feminist scholars, following the lead of Susan Brownmiller, contend that rape shows how deeply patriarchy is still entrenched. Men are encouraged to believe—through advertisements, movies, pornography—that women's bodies are their property. Others, like Andrea Dworkin, have argued that marital sex often turns into rape, even if not overtly violent, when husbands demand that their urges be satisfied. Maintaining power and control also explain why so many men are absorbed with being gratified orally, which features frequently in pornography. (Of course, women can and do enjoy this variant, either giving or receiving, but it doesn't seem to be nearly as much on their minds.)

Among biologists and anthropologists, there have always been some who insist that rape comes with the inherent condition of being male. Thus Michael Ghiglieri of the University of Northern Arizona reminds us that rape is "rampant" among scorpion flies, mallard ducks, and snow geese. And if it was common when our forebears lived in caves, we have to acknowledge that even in our more educated era, it has not gone away. Like male flies and geese, physical sex is crucial for men, so they may strew their genes to create the next generation. Hormones and synapses have evolved, which rouse men's passions and lead them to pursue women in hopes of creating a child. These deductions from Darwin 101 have won wide acceptance. But has evolution implanted a propensity for rape that lingers in modern men?

In Professor Ghiglieri's view, rape is a way of getting women pregnant when persuasion won't work. As he puts it, there will always be men who lack the "ability to attract desirable women through honest courtship." So they become "sexual predators," who seek to "steal copulation from unwilling women and thus increase their odds of siring offspring."

Should these speculations be taken seriously? Despite all the data about scorpion flies and prehistoric eras, in more modern times consensual sex has been sufficient to create successive generations of the human species. So our Darwinian reproduction has been achieved without resort to force. Doubtless some rapes result in births. But not all assaults include penetration; most emissions do not lead to pregnancies; and not all pregnancies end in live births. (Emergency rooms act quickly to apply spermicides, and even some archconservatives allow abortions for victims of rapes.) If rapists instinctively want to make babies bearing their genes, it can only be said that very few do, and even those offspring represent an insignificant share of the next generation.

With so much disagreement, it is probably best to steer clear of academic theorists. The typical rapist—if such a person exists—is surely impelled by a combination of sexual stirrings, anger, and sadism, plus an urge for power, and a conscious or unconscious wish to wreak sociopathic havoc. Rape is, after all, a form of terrorism.

FACTS AND FANTASIES

Nor do we have reliable evidence on whether we can reduce the incidence of rape or deter men who are drawn to it. Sensitivity sessions for high school students look impressive when we watch them being filmed; but one looks in vain for follow-ups on their subsequent effects. This is not to suggest that the propensity to rape is a trait inherent in some men. Every so often, scientists think they have found a gene—or the XYY chromosome—that can be linked to male aggression. But rape is a particular kind of violence; and thus far no one has identified a hereditary agent specific for that offense. (And if one is located, will all boys be tested for it before or after birth? And after that, what?)

Since rape is so coarse a crime, it is tempting to conclude that the men most apt to commit it have blue-collar employment, did poorly at school, and usually talk of women in scornful tones. Certainly when newspapers and television show arrested rapists, or sketches of suspects, the men tend to have a rough look. Indeed, we hardly ever hear of middle class men being charged with assault in public parks or deserted corners of garages. Men who work in offices are more often accused of hinting that sexual acquiescence will lead to employment preferment, or that it's necessary to keep a current job. But as this kind of harassment is rarely physically violent, it isn't recorded as rape if it is reported. Most men at executive and professional levels find it in their interest to suppress whatever cruder impulses they may have. They may be as tempted to rape as other men, but they know how much they would lose if they were arrested, or simply accused. Indeed, in this era of intrusive media, even wealthy families are no longer able to get the charges dropped, or to pay a victim to stay silent, as was often done.

We know what many men do when they feel a craving for violent sex. A segment of the pornography industry creates videos that simulate rape, with practiced professionals enacting scenarios they know their viewers want. Like those actors whose films were used in the experiments cited earlier, they are expert at faking brutal scenes, with time taken between shots to apply bogus cuts and bruises. In some of the movies, the women find that they like the roughness. This is better, they cry, than any sex they have had before, as if to say that it's right and proper for men to dominate women. That so many videos like these continue to be made and sell so well, as well as being popular on the Internet, must be taken as evidence that simulated rapes do something for the men watching them. (Along with projecting themselves onto the screens.)

Men with ampler wallets have an additional option. Much has been said and written about women who act as dominatrices. They are specialized professionals who bring to bear straps and chains and whips, all to gratify men with a yen for masochistic sex. Less heard about is another specialized group: women who agree to play the rape victim for clients willing to pay for an accomplished performance. Men seeking these services know how to scan coded advertisements in the raunchier magazines, and then detail what they want in subsequent telephone calls. While ground rules are set beforehand, the women still risk black eyes and bruises, even fractured bones. Just as some professionals serve masochistic men, others perform for sadists; which, after all, is what rapists are. More than a few men—we will never know how many—find that encounters like these work as sufficient substitutes for risking real rapes. But such services can cost $500 to $1,000, and are thus beyond the range of working-class men with similar urges. (Telephone-sex simulations are a lot cheaper; but less graphic and therefore less gratifying.)

From time to time, the fact that rape transcends class becomes apparent in the arrests of men from affluent backgrounds. Two such cases came to national view during the 1990s. One was William Kennedy Smith, who was tried for raping a woman at his family's Florida estate. The other was a young man named Alex Kelly, from a well-off Connecticut family, who fled to Europe for several years, but was convicted after he returned. In both trials, their lawyers argued that their clients were well-off and good-looking and had no need to rape, since they enjoyed no shortage of willing women. Hence their defense that the victims must have consented. Smith was acquitted, so this argument may have worked. However, Kelly was convicted despite his movie-star looks. And while athletic stars at colleges hardly lack for dates, every season finds some charged with unwanted sex. Perhaps they feel, as was apparently the case with Mike Tyson, that anyone who agrees to go out with them tacitly understands that the evening will end in bed.

VIEWS OF THE VICTIMS

Most men condemn the crime of rape, and express shock when incidents are reported. So when an arrest is made, men as well as women at first usually feel there must be something to the charge. At the same time, there have been mistaken accusations, or others with malicious motives. Everyone can recall such cases, not to mention stories or movies where the hero is targeted by a scorned or deranged woman.

So there can be signs of ambivalence, wherein questions about the victim crop up. In the Florida case of William Kennedy Smith, some people found themselves asking what a mother of two young children was doing in a bar past midnight. Or in the Mike Tyson case, why a pageant contestant accompanied him to his hotel room. Of course, those raising the doubts will claim they simply want more information. But also at issue is whether the women had exercised reasonable caution. And if they hadn't, didn't they share some of the burden for what ultimately happened? Women as well as men often find themselves wondering what the victim was wearing, whether she had had a few too many drinks, or was she flirting or sending signals that might have been misconstrued. This is not to suggest there is a wide presumption of innocence for men who have been indicted, but rather that victims cannot always expect complete sympathy. And if the accused has a vigorous lawyer, a woman who presses charges may find that she too is being tried.

Or part of the onus may be placed on women generally, more

particularly on the demeanor of many modern women. At issue here is an image of an idealized past when men respected women and treated them with care and consideration. In this rendering, members of the respective sexes knew their natural roles, wherein each had specified rights and accepted mutual obligations. The problem for many men today is that women are challenging them as never before, with demands for full equality, as well as rivaling them in fitness and agility. As a result, at least some men have come to believe that women no longer want or need traditional protections. Again, this neither justifies nor excuses rape, but affects the way assaults are perceived.

RATIONALIZING RAPE

The question that opened this chapter was why rape persists, especially in a society that prides itself on being enlightened and civilized. In fact, we have no way of knowing whether sexual crimes have been increasing or decreasing over the years. Such records and statistics as we have are incomplete or questionable or combine different kinds of incidents. What we do know is that serious sexual crimes continue and show no sign of abating.

Regarding how many man have engaged in coerced sex, we have seen estimates ranging from tens of thousands to tens of millions. But whatever the real number, there are enough of them to blemish the texture of society. What will follow are some speculations on who these men are and why they behave as they do.

Of course, people who perpetrate identical acts can do so for different reasons. This is the view of many researchers who study rape. Thus a study prepared for the New York Academy of Sciences emphasized the "need to examine multi-motivational themes and how they are lived out in the offenses." This view was based on an examination of 201 convicted rapists in the Massachusetts prison system, including testimony at their trials, sentencing reports, and interviews with the inmates. They concluded that the reasons why men rape fall under five major headings, acknowledging that there can be overlapping and that other scholars have used other categories. Based on their sample, these are the major motivations:

Opportunistic (23 percent). Here men find themselves in situations where rape becomes possible, and it occurs. This is what happens in most date rapes. In a typical scenario, either or both in the party may have too much to drink, and one or both may become sexually stimulated. But at a certain juncture, she tells him to stop; however, he holds her down and proceeds despite her protests. In such cases, sex is what he chiefly wants: to release a pressure that has been growing all evening. These are the least damaging kinds of rapes, at least in the view of the researchers, since there is "little anger or unnecessary violence."

Compensatory (25 percent). These men tend to be loners, often with "low self-esteem and pervasive feelings of inadequacy." They compensate by conjuring up fantasies in which they are loved and desired. In these inventions, even if he rapes a woman—indeed, because he has—she will become affectionate. In at least a few cases, this delusion has such a hold that he endeavors to see her again. (In turn, she often tells the police and helps them make an arrest.)

Displaced Anger (11 percent). These are men filled with hate and fury, and generally angry at the world. They can and do hate other men, but reserve most of their resentment for women. In some cases, their victim serves as a surrogate for their mother. But just as commonly, their rancor responds to "a cumulative series of experienced or imagined insults from many women."

Exploitative (32 percent). These men are also vindictive, but their animus is specifically toward women. For them, it tends to be "an impulsive, predatory act," which is not planned beforehand, but takes advantage of "immediate" opportunities. But once they embark, their aim is to humiliate, degrade, and destroy the women chosen as their victims. Still, insofar as they commit successive rapes, they are engaged in a war against the entire opposite sex.

Sadistic (8 percent). These men, to a greater extent than the others, revel in brutality. Their fantasies never involve love, but rather feature pain, maiming, even death. For them, there evolves "a synergistic relationship between sexual and aggressive drives," where the sex itself becomes a belligerent act. In the end he wants her to feel soiled and degraded, indeed that thought provides much of his pleasure.

There comes a point, though, when less is more. Yes, we know most subjects are complicated and have many intersecting forces, so all generalization should be suspect. But on the subject of this chapter, there comes a time when more understanding is gained by ascertaining what all rapists have in common than by parsing them into categories.

This said, the view to be taken here is that men who rape—and many who fantasize doing it—both hate and fear women. Not just some specific women, but all members of that sex. A lot of men feel this way, including many who deny it, but those who rape are prepared to translate their feelings into action. Some select their victims almost at random; regardless of who the woman is, she represents her sex. Others vent their anger at a particular woman: someone they feel has insulted or demeaned them, or has not deferred to them in ways they feel they deserve. In their view, this haughty air is especially endemic among women who feel they are attractive or smart or the equals of men. These kinds of sentiments are felt by those who rape while on a date and others who pick their victims on impulse and still others who stalk and stake out strangers.

If rape is brutal, most rapists are brutes. Of course, not all are burly or brawny. But what all have in common is a readiness, if not an eagerness, to beat and batter women, to punch and pummel them. Rapists do not say, "please"; nor do they ask, "may I?" They get their way by threatening or in fact inflicting physical pain. Much, probably most, of their pleasure comes from the terror they evoke. So being willing to assault someone smaller than one's self is something they look forward to—probably dream about—doing. Of course, rape has a sexual component. But its pleasure is often an aftermath, since another gratification, the one from wreaking physical and emotional anguish, is their first wish.

All rapists aim at inflicting scars on their victims, imprints they will carry for the rest of their lives. They want their rape to be a stigma, designed to devalue the woman in the regard of others, all the better if it ruins her relationship with a husband or fiancé. In these and other ways, the rapist feels he is acting on behalf of all members of his sex, since he is persuaded that they share his hostility toward women, even as they lack his courage to put them in their place. They are the counterparts of terrorists, a dedicated minority who enlist in a cause, and thus have an impact far beyond their numbers.

The effect rapists desire is to undermine an enemy. While not all women will experience this trauma, enough do so the threat can cow an entire gender. If all women are held in thrall, the rapist believes, men can reclaim the dominance they are in danger of losing. Indeed, women have always threatened men, since the days of Circe and Delilah and Jezebel. So in the rapist's mind, there will always be a need for men like him. True, women do not spend all their waking hours quaking in mortal fear. Yet, together, the precautions they feel they should observe set constraints around their lives. They include where one may prudently walk, or even drive; how or whether to respond to a conversational overture. While such safeguards may reflect a general fear of crime, anxiety over rape is never far from the surface. And that this stress is always there is a victory for the men who wield it as a weapon.

9

Homosexuality:
An Emerging Alternative

In this chapter, too, we will be considering some sensititve subjects on which people can have strong opinions and there is little agreement on fundamental facts. Early in the book, it was proposed that marriages work best if the partners have what were called "complementary temperaments." While this is a beguiling ideal, rising divorce rates suggest it's not one that many couples have been able to attain. Nor is it simply that people are making inappropriate choices. There is a real possibility that fewer men and women have the dispositions to live with someone of the other sex.

In addition, until fairly recently, it was widely assumed that nearly everyone was heterosexual, and this was the only normal and natural identity men and women could have. Some took this reasoning even further, adding that if persons said they weren't heterosexual, they were either deluding themselves or acting out a personal problem. Needless to say, there are still individuals who think this way.

The assumption of heterosexuality easily combined with the premise that the sexes had a natural affinity. Thus, in theory, equal numbers of men and women would be available for pairing off. And in the past, this happened to a remarkable degree. After all, that was what society expected. Men and women proceeded to oblige, including some who found themselves attracted to members of their own sex. As a result, nineteen of every twenty women received marriage proposals they were willing to accept. In 1980, the Census asked all adults if they had ever been wed. (This question is no longer asked.) Among those

137

who were in their fifties that year, 94.2 percent of the men had married at least once, as had 95.3 percent of the women. There is little likelihood that figures this high will be reached again.

One reason is that the presumption of heterosexuality is no longer made. But that would not be such a problem, if equal numbers of men and women were choosing another option. If this were the case, they too could pair off with people who share their orientation, just as heterosexuals do. However, the heterosexual numbers tell another story. While we have no firm figures, all indications are that about three times as many men are identifying themselves as gay as there are women embracing a lesbian designation. As a result, there are fewer heterosexual men available for pairing with the women who share that affinity. Thus we hear from many women the complaint that many men they initially find attractive turn out not to be sexually available. This chapter will endeavor to explain the reasons for this imbalance. Here, as in other areas, we will rely on statistics as far as we can, and then proceed further into speculative terrain.

Despite the uncertainty about actual figures, it is obvious that millions of men and women are asserting, without diffidence or hesitation, that *being* homosexual is a valid depiction of who and what they are. In so doing, they are saying that this is how they are physically and emotionally composed. They often add that this orientation reflects their genetic makeup; that they were programmed this way at conception; and it is inherent in their identity. Whether homosexuality is encapsulated in a specific gene or chromosome has yet to be determined. But it won't be wholly surprising if such discoveries are eventually made.

For many years, it was widely thought that homosexuality stemmed from experiences an individual might have had while growing up. This opinion was based on the idea, cited earlier, that all human beings are naturally heterosexual. Therefore, people who are gay or lesbian would feel this way because they had been exposed to influences regarded as perverted or unnatural. This remains part of the concern about adults who try to beguile young people into homosexual activity. There is the fear that these seducers are also recruiters, seeking to turn an initiation into a lifetime conversion.

Another explanation focused on boys who grew up in families

where the mother was the dominant parent. As a result. these men remain so tied to their mothers that they could not form attachments to other women. This theory informs Dorothy Dinnerstein's theory that if fathers were to become more active in childrearing, fewer sons would end up believing they are homosexuals.

Still another idea comes from Betty Jean Lifton, who says that in her practice as a psychotherapist she found that children who have been adopted are more likely to be homosexual. Adopted women, she says, may identify as lesbians since they feel "hostile to men because they imagine their fathers deserted their mothers." For a boy, she adds, knowing that he was not a "real son" can be the "ultimate emasculating experience." This leads to displaying demeanors that could be considered "feminine." (In fact, it isn't clear that most gay men take on such traits; indeed many make a point of being muscular and masculine.) Conclusions like these are typically propounded by therapists, who cite patients who have come to them with sex-related problems. There is no reason to doubt that some children who were adopted later conclude they are homosexual. But whether the one condition causes the other is far from proven. The Census estimated in 2000 that 700,000 children were living with adoptive parents, and several times that number will now be adults. So we need to know whether disproportionate numbers of people in this group are or will be members of the gay or lesbian community.

The real issue is whether homosexuality is induced by experiences that some people may have but others don't. It was once proposed that its prevalence among English upper-class men stemmed from their being whipped ("caned") on the buttocks during their years at boarding school. There are also some conservatives who still believe that homosexuality is a mental illness, and that this presumed impairment can be "cured" by appropriate treatment. (Until 1973, the American Psychiatric Association as much as propounded that view in its diagnostic manual.) Persons who still hold to this idea like to cite instances where, as they view it, therapy has brought individuals back to heterosexuality. (Most homosexuals will assert they were never there to begin with.) While such cases may exist, they are far outweighed by the many men and women who are sure that they are gay or lesbian and have no desire to change that orientation.

THE SCOPE OF SEXUALITY

Some men and women who believe they are homosexual, or have begun to suspect this is so, keep these intimations to themselves. They may be married and raising children and wish to preserve these relationships. (From time to time, they may have liaisons with someone of their own sex, in some cases with their spouse's knowledge.) Moreover, homoerotic acts are not confined to people who identify themselves as gay or lesbian. Most notably, these occur among prison inmates—sometimes consensual, often not—who cease such sexual activity after completing their sentences. Many young people experiment with others of their own sex; but for most of them, these episodes do not change their conviction that they are fully heterosexual.

Men who regard themselves as heterosexual are generally more adamant than women in asserting that this is their sole identity. The possibility that they could be sexually attracted to other men is something they work hard to suppress and repress. Note the vehemence with which men who pride themselves on their masculinity try to distance themselves from the gay portion of the population. The amount of ridicule that can still be heard when straight men are together is revealing and makes one wonder why their targets are accorded so much attention. As we know, hostility is usually a mask for fear. It seems likely that those who are so preoccupied are struggling with homoerotic impulses within themselves, which they faintly recognize and are trying to obliterate. If this view is consistent with common sense, it also has science on its side, as shown by an experiment that was reported in the *Journal of Abnormal Psychology*:

From feelings they expressed about homosexuals, 35 men were identified as *homophobic*. Another 29 were deemed to be *nonhomophobic,* from their responses about gays and being gay. All 64 agreed to watch explicit videotapes of heterosexual and homosexual sex; and, while doing so, to have a "circumferential strain gauge" placed on their penis. Thus if their member became aroused, its degree of enlargement would be calibrated by a device that was described in the chapter on rape, the versatile *penile plethysmograph*. Both groups showed about the same level of arousal while watching the heterosexual videos. But during the homosexual video, 54 percent of the homophobic men registered "definite tumescence," whereas only 24 percent of the nonphobic men did. They were also asked verbally if the homosexual video turned them on. Most of the phobic men said it hadn't, even though their plethysmographs had recorded otherwise. Could it just possibly be that the men were seeing themselves in the scenes on the screen?

But experiments like these do not show that men who make much of their masculinity are repressed homosexuals. The study's sample also reminds us that not all men are homophobic. Yet even those who don't show hostility are still firm about their being heterosexual. Moreover, being open-minded is often accompanied by fascination with the style and structure of gay life, a curiosity that may conceal a latent attraction. This noted, a basic theme of this chapter is that no one is exclusively heterosexual or homosexual. Nor is anything gained by saying we are both. We are simply *sexual* creatures. The modifiers *"homo"* and *"hetero"* do not designate inborn affinities. Rather, they are descriptions that people have accepted, chosen, or had thrust upon them. They are also indications of your place in society, in the same way you might identify yourself as a Presbyterian or a Methodist, or a Democrat or a Republican.

Still, opinions can be revealing because they affect how people behave and what they make of the world. Almost all gay men and committed lesbians are sure that their orienation is inherent within themselves, and is as innate as the color of their eyes. When heterosexual women are asked for their views on the causes of homosexuality, they tend to divide evenly on genetic versus family or social causes. Yet straight men cite aspects of upbringing by a margin of more than two to one. So to their professed certainty about their heterosexual identity, they add the view that being gay is not genetic. And this then allows them to assert that gay men need not be that way. While, we should always be careful about ascribing defensiveness and denial to others, it is at least worth pondering if these men suspect that they may be carrying some homosexual genes themselves, a possibility they would rather not confront. The best way to erase their own unease is to assert that being gay is a choice, which can always be rescinded or reversed. So they are basically saying to homosexuals: *you really don't have to be that way.*

ARE WOMEN MORE AMBIVALENT?

The nationwide sex survey cited in some earlier chapters found 1.4 percent of the women that were interviewed said they were lesbian, whereas 2.6 percent of the men admitted to being homosexual. The actual numbers for both sexes are undoubtedly higher, since not everyone is ready to reveal their orientation. (Other studies have put the male figure at as high as 7 to 8 percent.) Still, given the figures we have, it remains to explain the imbalance. There may be one, very simple, cause. Accepting the premise that homosexuality is genetic, it need not be assumed that nature has distributed these imprints in the sexes in equal proportions. Just as some temperaments are more evident in one sex, so may be a propensity to claim a distinct sexual identity. Or it may be that most cultures allow women more flexibility in expressing their sexual side.

On the whole, women are less constrained than men when it comes to expressing their affections. While a relatively small number consider themselves to be lesbians, most routinely act in ways that men usually associate with that term. Thus they kiss and caress close women friends, hold hands, and affirm their love and fellow feeling. In fact, this isn't being "lesbian," or even "bisexual"; they are normal and natural signs of fondness. As a result, fewer women feel a need to declare themselves as lesbians, since they are already able to convey their closeness to members of their own sex. If straight men also allowed themselves to behave this way with other men, it might be that fewer of them would feel compelled to conclude that they are solely homosexual.

Nor do such displays undercut the attachments women have felt for men in their lives. They have found that being close to other women does not conflict with seeing themselves as essentially heterosexual. Several movie scenarios show paths women can take in seeking their sexual identity. In *Lianna* (1983), a wife who is fed up with her philandering husband finds herself in bed with another woman, although that relationship proves to be transitory. While she never declares herself to be a lesbian, by the end of the film, she is moving in with a woman who promises to be a congenial companion. The heroine of *Chasing Amy* (1997) is cast as a confirmed lesbian whose friends look to her for leadership and support. But then she falls in love with a man, and the film ends with them together. However, she refrains from saying that she has become heterosexual. And in *Kissing Jessica Stein* (2002), the single heroine is shown regarding all the men she meets as creeps or worse. So she embarks on a romance with an avowed lesbian. But the relationship falls apart, because the lover wants her to redefine herself, which Jessica is unwilling to do. The movie ends with the heroine musing about dating men again, particularly an old flame. Or to move from fantasy to fact, consider the experience of the actress Anne Heche, who broke up with her lover Ellen DeGeneres, and shortly afterward married a cameraman named Coleman Laffoon. The singer Sinead O'Connor, who acknowledges having had partners of both sexes, wed a journalist named Nicholas Sommerlad. Whether in films or in reality, one would have to look hard to find men who have taken similar paths.

Many of the women who do describe themselves as lesbians were once married and often have children. At some point, they began to feel that another woman would make a more companionable partner. Other women may embark on such relationships, but still refrain from declaring a new identity, as was seen in the movie scenarios. While enthralled with their new lovers, they aren't sure they want to confine all their subsequent choices to a single sex. This is also the case among college women who are responding to sexual imbalances on campuses by choosing to be, as they put it, "gay until graduation." This kind of indeterminacy is rare among men. For example, homosexuals who were once married usually insist there is no way they could return to being heterosexual.

Frank Furstenberg of the University of Pennsylvania, one of the foremost scholars of the interactions between the sexes, poses a question to the students in his classes. He asks them to imagine that they will be on a desert island for several months and can have only one companion, a randomly chosen person of about their own age. Would you pick a man or a woman? He gave the students a weekend to think it over, and told them they could discuss the question with friends if they liked. When they came back with their answers, it turned out that almost every man in the class—as far as Furstenberg knew, they were all heterosexual—said that he would prefer a woman for his island-mate. And few showed any hesitation about coming to that decision. As for the women, most declared that they would want it to be another woman.

To understand their reasoning, Furstenberg then talked at some length with the students. The men were thinking about having a steady sexual partner, while few women gave this high priority and many never mentioned it at all. The men also expected that a woman would be supportive during a lonely period, and seemed to assume that as the man, they would be in charge. The women's responses showed that they envisioned becoming friends with their female companion, and so could ameliorate an isolating experience with continuing conversations. And since the women would be with someone of their gender, they expected that the relationship would be on an equal plane. On the other hand, were she alone with a man, she would be expected to devote much of her energy to taking care of his needs.

Both homosexual and heterosexual men insist that the sexual designations that apply to them fully describe their identities. Why are they so adamant? The simplest explanation comes from what they have in common: they are men. On the whole, men are less willing to live with ambiguity, or what on the surface seems to be inconsistency. This was seen in chapter 7, regarding the efforts made to mask the fragility of masculinity. Women are more at ease with anomalies—if that is what they are—not only about the world, but also concerning themselves, not least their sexual identities.

AN ADDITIONAL IMBALANCE

The designations *homosexual* and *heterosexual* show how people think of themselves, and to that extent they become a reality in the minds of millions of individuals. (The same could be said about race.) By all outward indicators, more Americans than ever before are now willing to say they are gay or lesbian, or allow others to make that inference. The big shift from the past is among young people coming of sexual age, many more of whom feel able to avow being gay both to themselves and the world.

If the gay population seems to be on the rise, the easiest explanation is that more people are coming out. Let's look, for example, at men aged 40 to 44 in 2000, who were reaching adulthood at a time when disclosing being gay was gaining acceptance. As can seen in the table on the next page, the proportion of men in this age range who had never been married by 2000 has more doubled since 1970, rising from 7.5 percent to 15.8 percent. The latter figure is noteworthy, even allowing for the later ages at which people are now marrying. While some of these bachelors obviously think of themselves as heterosexual, the fact is that few straight men haven't married at least once by the time they reach their forties. In the most recent tabulations, less than two percent of first-time grooms had put it off that long.

But men who stay bachelors comprise only part of the picture. The table also shows that among men aged 40 to 44, the proportion who were divorced and had not remarried leaped from 3.8 percent in 1970 to 13.2 percent in 2000, over a threefold increase. In an earlier chapter, it was suggested that divorced heterosexual men generally remarry, usually quite soon, because they feel bereft without a "nest." This would seem especially true among those who get divorced in their forties, which is a bit late for mastering domestic arts. But the growth of the divorced-and-not-remarried group suggests that it now contains a number of *homosexual* men who were once married, and will not be doing so again. (Or cannot, until a lot of laws are changed.) In 1970, most homosexual men who had married stayed with that arrangement, since coming out was much more hazardous than it is today.

So why have as many as 15.8 percent of all men in their early forties not chosen to marry at all, and what about the additional 13.2 percent who are divorced and have not remarried? Together, they total 29.0 percent, almost one in three of men this age, the highest such proportion in the nation's history. In 1970, by way of contrast, bachelors and divorced men who hadn't remarried together made up only 11.3 percent of men in the same age range.

MARRIED AND OTHERWISE

	1970	Men Aged 40–44	2000	
	84.2%	Currently Married	66.3%	
	3.7%	Separated	4.2%	
8.3%	3.8%	Divorced	13.2%	17.9%
	0.8%	Widowed	0.5%	
	7.5%	Never Married	15.8%	
	100.0%		100.0%	

	1970	Women Aged 40–44	2000	
	80.4%	Currently Married	66.4%	
	4.9%	Separated	5.3%	
14.2%	5.6%	Divorced	15.0%	21.8%
	3.7%	Widowed	1.5%	
	5.4%	Never Married	11.8%	
	100.0%		100.0%	

The most plausible explanation for so sharp an increase is that more men are discovering they are gay, either early or later on, and are deciding to act outwardly on this knowledge rather than pretending to be heterosexual. Does this mean that male homosexuality is more prevalent than in the past, and not just that more men are coming out? This question can't be easily answered, since it's impossible to get head counts from the past. We do know that nature is constantly changing distributions within species, including the human variant, and just might be creating more people with homosexual inclinations. On how a gay population will reproduce itself, some donate sperm to assist women friends. But the best answer is that it can count on its next generation coming from heterosexual parents, as has always been the case.

The table also shows distributions for women. Between 1970 and

2000, those in their early forties who were unmarried or had once been married rose from 19.6 percent to 33.6 percent. The future will see a decrease in heterosexual matches, since women who prefer male partners are finding fewer men who want to pair with a woman. In this respect, women in general are experiencing a situation that black women have been facing for quite some time: what has been called "the man shortage." This phenomenon, and others related to race, will be explored in the next chapter.

ANOTHER ALTERNATIVE: BEYOND EITHER/OR

From time to time, we hear of individuals who wish to describe themselves as *bisexual*. To have meaning, this designation should signify not just having had one or two experiences. Instead, it expresses a man or woman's firmly held belief that gender simply does not matter to them when they consider prospective partners. Thus far bisexuality hasn't been attributed to genes or associated with upbringing, and it may be more a preference rather than a full-fledged identity. Still, its outlook was conveyed by a guest at a wedding—gender not specified—who was supposedly overheard to say of the bride and groom:

> They're a charming couple.
> I've slept with both of them.

It would probably be just as well not to regard bisexuality as a third and separate category. Indeed, it may well be that it is what all of us are. If we are honest with ourselves—which is a lot to ask—all of us might admit that we are capable of being physically attracted to individuals of either sex. In fact, this was Sigmund Freud's view. He used the word "polymorphous," to suggest we can express ourselves sexually in many ways, and need not limit our partners to a particular gender. That is where both heterosexuality and homosexuality are needlessly confining, since both set fully half of humanity off bounds as possible dates or mates or spouses. If this view has enough plausibility to deserve some pondering, it challenges ingrained sentiments about what is moral and natural.

"Polymorphous" clearly connotes a plurality of possibilities. And the human condition has already contrived a wide variety of ways to express and release sexuality. For example, some of the more popular pornographic productions that men like to watch are those showing two women together. To which may be added not unknown occasions when a husband suggests to his wife that another woman join them. Or where he asks if he can watch while she is with another man.

It may be that the prospect of endless sexual possibilities is more than most of us can handle. Suppression and repression are not wholly irrational if the alternative is uncertainty and confusion, as well as doing damage to others and inflicting harm on ourselves.

10

The Black Experience:
A Portent for Whites

In 1965, a young official in the U.S. Department of Labor named Daniel Patrick Moynihan released a report entitled *The Negro Family: The Case for National Action.* His analysis was brutal. Black households, he said, were caught in a "tangle of pathology." To support this contention, his report was full of tables, graphs, and statistics. Moynihan lamented that "nearly one-quarter of Negro births are now illegitimate," while "almost one-fourth of Negro families are headed by females." By way of contrast, he cited his own race. "The white family," he wrote, "has achieved a high degree of stability and is maintaining that stability." As evidence, he noted that the rate for white out-of-wedlock births was only one eighth of that recorded for the black population.

Today, we still hear a lot about the divide between the races. But in at least one respect, the gap is closing. White families are no longer being congratulated for their *stability.* Divorce, decamping fathers, and births to unmarried women are nearly as common in white suburbs as they once were in the predominantly black inner cities. In fact, one could now propose to undertake a study called *The White Family: A Tangle of Pathology.*[*]

Of course, much has been said about the state of families in general.

---

[*]In fact, growing numbers of Americans are regarded as neither *black* nor *white.* Hispanics, Asians, American Indians, Hawaiians, and others are not regarded as races, but are identified by their geographic origins and cultural traditions.

However, Moynihan focused on race, and his emphasis remains relevant today. So we need to remember that America has two principal races, and one of them is white. But it is revealing that when the behavior of white people falls short of accepted standards, their conduct is not viewed as having a racial basis. (For example, no one does research on *white* drug abuse, or asks why insider traders and serial killers are almost always white.) That so many white families are no longer showing Moynihan's "stability" is worth emphasizing, if only because their race has always congratulated itself on its commitment to keeping families strong and durable.

THE FLIGHT OF WHITE FATHERS

As the decade-by-decade table on this page shows, since 1960 fewer men—black or white—are staying with the women they married and the children they fathered. This is significant, because white Americans have felt free to criticize what they saw as a lack of discipline on the part of their black fellow citizens. Beyond that, welfare

A MAN IN THE HOUSE?

*Families with Children**

Percentage Headed by Married Couples

White		Black
90.9%	1960	67.0%
88.7%	1970	64.1%
85.1%	1980	55.0%
82.9%	1990	46.8%
79.8%	2000	43.8%

*Marriages include those with stepparents.

rolls have been slashed and allowances were suspended to halt what was seen as irresponsible procreation among much of the black population. In addition, Americans of European ancestry have prided themselves on their demanding standards. From colonial days, they made a point of proclaiming their devotion to duties associated with marriage and parenthood. And by adhering to this ethic, they have felt entitled to lecture others for their failings. How ironic, then, to look at the decreasing number of white households headed by a married couple.

By 2000, this number was 79.8 percent. However, not all those men were the children's fathers. About a tenth were stepfathers, usually a man the mother had married after an earlier divorce. Some stepfathers are attentive and caring, and may even adopt the children, if the biological father consents. But the fact is that most of these stepfamilies do not last. All told, then, only about 70 percent of white homes now have both the biological parents in residence. So this 2000 figure puts white households close to where their black counterparts were in 1960, when they were described as "a tangle of pathology."

The table also shows that only 43.8 percent of black families have resident husbands, or about 40 percent if only biological parents are counted. As is evident, this decline continues to be precipitous, and is a cause for concern. Unlike most of the white households, the paucity of husbands in black families reflects the fact that over half the women who head them were not married in the first place.

The reasons why so many black fathers are absent has been debated for several decades. One contention is that this is a legacy of slavery, when durable relationships were discouraged, even destroyed, by the system. In fact, the sanctions imposed by the owners were never accepted by the slaves themselves. Once freed, they sought the unions they had been denied. For almost a century after the Civil War, black families remained remarkably stable. Despite low incomes and uncertain employment, most black households had two parents in residence, even if bound by common-law marriages.

A more plausible explanation is that by 1960, the economy had begun to eliminate the kinds of jobs that allowed black men to be steady earners for their families. The movement from Southern farms to Northern cities, which started in the 1940s, was spurred by industrial expansion and accompanied by the emergence of labor unions. However, that era of well-paid factory jobs did not last long. First, companies moved to the suburbs, and then began to have their manufacturing done overseas. As office jobs came to predominate, black men were not considered for these positions. And the next generation, still confined for the most part to inner cities, was not being prepared for college and white-collar employment. In the last four decades, millions of black men have been shut out of the mainstream economy. All too many became fathers, at least in the nominal sense, with little prospect of ever having the resources to become full-time resident parents.

White men, however, can't cite reasons like these for leaving their marriages and children. Even if the slavery theory were valid, it obviously doesn't apply to people whose ancestors came here voluntarily, and were never chained as chattels. That leaves the explanation based on a changing economy and the disappearance of decent jobs. True, some white men grow up in discouraging surroundings and end up with low incomes or none at all. There are even Yale graduates who never quite make it.

This may be true, but the fact remains that one of the great achievements of the second half of the last century was to virtually erase the class of poor white people. Those who had been raised in urban slums were able to move to suburbs, where their children attended schools that ushered them into white-collar occupations. Others left small towns for opportunities elsewhere, and in time saw their children at state universities. The nation's back roads may still be home to decaying trailer parks, with worn tires in front yards. The men there may be pretty rough; but most are regularly employed, not least because they have buddies who pass on the word about tolerable jobs.

According to the 2000 Census, among white men aged 35 to 44, only 38.4 percent had incomes under $35,000. So the other 61.6 percent made enough to be modest providers for families. For black men that age, the figures were almost exactly the reverse: 61.4 percent had paychecks under $35,000, while only 38.6 percent made over that figure. This racial pay gap is not trivial. It shows, as well as any index, that even 135 years after the end of the Civil War, the economy has yet to allow equal opportunities to descendants of slaves. Moreover, these percentages do not include almost a million black men who are currently imprisoned, and thus entirely removed from the job market.

There are endless arguments about why so many black men end up near the bottom of the earnings scale. Conservatives stress that it's due to a lack of hard work and attempts at self-improvement. A more convincing explanation is that racial discrimination continues to be a central fact in American employment. Despite the requisite denials, most of those charged with hiring and promoting are still not fully persuaded that men of African ancestry have the talents needed for the positions to be filled. White men do not find a similar suspicion directed at their race.* Nor can they say they were relegated to inferior schools and unpromising neighborhoods because they were of European origins.

MEN'S LIBERATION REVISITED

If nothing else, the figures on page 150 attest to a growing unwillingness by white men to become or remain resident fathers to the children they have sired. In an earlier chapter, this was called *men's liberation,* signaling a flight from obligations that once bound members of their race and sex. Of course, it can't be shown that they were murmuring to themselves, *"If black men can do it, why shouldn't I?"* All the same, rates for whites began to change at a time when Norman Mailer was heralding *The White Negro,* when movies like *Shaft* glamorized black potency, and the vogue for Elvis Presley's rock and roll reveled in its black origins. Whether due to causation or coincidence, a new wave of white men decided to cut loose. Moreover, many of these departing fathers were comfortably middle class, indeed often affluent. So they couldn't claim that prejudice and employment barriers made it difficult for them to support their families.

Indeed, the changing demeanor of white men begins even before they embark on fatherhood. In 2000, only 43.3 percent of whites who

* Some may say they were passed over due to affirmative action programs. But even if this happened, they were not regarded as having lesser qualifications than the people who were given the jobs.

received bachelor's degrees were men. By way of contrast, in 1976, when racial statistics were first published, their figure was 54.2 percent. This is a notable change because throughout this period, most white youths continued to be raised in stable homes and to attend schools with college preparatory programs. Yet each year more of these young men turn away from academic pursuits. This concern has been commonly voiced about black youths who end their education with high school. While it cannot be proved that white youths purposely copy their black counterparts, the figures show that in attitudes on schooling, racial lines are blurring.

HIP-HOP AND BASKETBALL

As has been remarked in other chapters, there are times when we need explanations, but evidence is not easily obtained or is nonexistent. What will follow are further conjectures about the behavior of white men. These observations obviously aren't scientific, and can be challenged for lacking factual foundations. Yet some statistics can serve as starting points. One is that over 70 percent of rap recordings are bought by white teenagers, almost all of whom are boys. Another is that about 85 percent of the seats at college and professional basketball games are filled with white fans, the great majority of whom are men.

Rap and hip-hop music began in the inner city and reflects the aura and attitudes of a segregated America. Of course, it has a core of black buyers, who are usually the first to identify new talents. What is seldom remarked is that the bulk of the market for hip-hop consists of white teenagers who live in comfortable suburbs. And it is due to their purchases that a recording reaches platinum levels. Clearly this kind of music has a resonance for these high schoolers. It gives them a window into a strident and assertive world, unfettered by inhibitions, where sex is sovereign and women are there to be used. Just possibly, too, they turn it up to torture their parents. And there are now *white* rap groups, like Eminem and Beastie Boys, who have spurred a crossover from the ghetto to gated communities. Here, as before, it will only be noted that rap's arrival in the suburbs coincided with a growing disaffection from education. And it may also be coincidental that its stress on hit-and-run sex came just as white men were excusing themselves from obligations of fatherhood.

In recent decades, basketball has outpaced all other sports in rising attendance and public attention. The reasons are easy to understand. Basketball players display a grace and elegance seldom seen in athletes, whether performing as individuals or as a team. It wasn't always so. Until World War II, professional basketball teams would only recruit white players, and by all accounts this resulted in a lackluster game. The breaking of that barrier brought new infusions of talent. Within just a few years, professional and college teams had become predominantly black, and the sport began to shine.*

Look at the audience in any basketball arena, and you will see predominantly white men cheering on the players they regard as comprising *their* teams. This expression of identity can be construed in several ways. In one sense, these fans feel that the team belongs to them, either as college alumni or the residents of a particular city. (The teams' owners foster this illusion, since it helps fill seats.) But there is another reason. It is worth noting that these fans are mainly white, many of them not in prime condition. Why are they cheering so avidly for those statuesque young black men on the court? Simply stated, what these white spectators see are images of their primal selves: the men they once were or might have been, had not Caucasian evolution taken another track. While not consciously realized, the players represent an aboriginal manhood not repressed by the constraints of modern life. In rooting for *their* teams, white fans can fantasize about becoming one with them, even as they realize that their sedentary commitments render that return impossible. And, to add a line from the chapter on masculinity, the white men in the stands may be hoping to emulate the sexual prowess attributed to black athletes. Of all basketball statistics, among the most remembered is Wilt Chamberlain's claim to having slept with 20,000 women. And that the players tend to be superbly built, are sparsely clad, and gleam with sweat, raises issues that were discussed in the chapter on homosexuality.

*A new development has been the recruitment of white players from Europe and Asia. Whether this will change the racial ambience of basketball will soon be seen.

WHITE AND OUT-OF-WEDLOCK

In 1950, when the baby boom was getting under way and young white families were starting to move to the suburbs, fewer than two percent of white births were to unmarried women. As previously mentioned, some obliging doctors probably recorded other births as occurring at seven months. But since they were sanctified by hasty marriages, these babies were considered "legitimate." The figures in the table on this page can be interpreted in several ways. One is that the ratio of births to single black women has grown fourfold during the last five decades, continuing the trend Moynihan wrote about. But during this period, the rate for whites rose by thirteen times, or three times as much as it rose for blacks. Or, as the table also shows, the white rate has moved from a 9.9 multiple of the black ratio down to 3.1. And as can be seen, the 2000 white percentage is higher than the black rate for 1960, which was condemned in Moynihan's report. This is graphic evidence of racial convergence, and again raises the question why white women appear to be emulating their black counterparts.

It is worth recalling that, taken together, the white women come from more affluent backgrounds, and have higher earnings when they are older. Thus there has been a class shift in unmarried motherhood,

ON THEIR OWN

Births to Unmarried Women

	White	Black	Ratio
1950	1.7	16.8%	9.9
1960	2.3%	21.6%	9.4
1970	5.7%	37.6%	6.6
1980	9.3%	56.4%	6.1
1990	16.9%	66.7%	3.9
2001	22.5%	68.3%	3.0

and it is no longer a province of the poor. Moreover, the age distributions for the two races are virtually identical: about 28 percent of the mothers are in their teens; about 57 percent are in their twenties; while the remaining 15 percent are older. Another similarity is that 15.9 percent of the white mothers have attended college, which is not far from the 18.3 percent for black mothers.

An additional factor, which was noted in an earlier chapter, is that almost all these births are voluntary. That is, the number of girls and women who cannot find abortion facilities, and are forced to have children they definitely do not want, make up a small fraction of the total. True, this is not a subject on which it is easy to obtain statistics. Still, a 1995 survey by the Department of Health and Human Services found nearly half—45.1 percent—of pregnant single women declaring they were "happy" about their condition, which suggests they were looking forward to the birth. It seems valid to presume that most of the other women who didn't feel that way had abortions, since at least a million of each year's abortion patients are unmarried.

Some people feel that having an out-of-wedlock child is a frivolous or capricious act, an ego-driven decision by the mother and ultimately harmful to the youngster. As was shown in earlier chapters, it is certainly true that children residing only with their mother will have lower standards of living and face hurdles unknown to their counterparts in more affluent homes. However, unmarried women can want to become mothers just as much as those who are happily married. Bearing a child is a right as well as a pleasure; and if one had to pass a test for motherhood, it isn't clear that all married women would get passing grades. What can be suggested, though, is that our society is depending on these non-marital births to provide a considerable portion of the next generation.

Let's suppose, for a moment, that in the year 2000, the only births had been to married couples. Instead of 622,598 black infants, there would only have been 195,949. And instead of 2,362,968 white births, the number would have fallen to 1,841,282. Had this occurred, not only would neither race be reproducing itself, but there will be many fewer Americans to serve in the workforce that will be needed in the decades ahead.

MOTHERHOOD ON YOUR OWN

In the past, it was mainly black women who either chose or accepted single motherhood, largely because they faced a shortage of men who would be constant or reliable husbands. Recently, more and more white women have been reaching a similar conclusion. As was seen, fewer white men are continuing with their education, and in time we will see how far this will affect their earning power. Some may make decent incomes in fields like construction and computer systems. And there will certainly still be enough educated men to become corporate officers, investment bankers, and the best-paid neurosurgeons. Even so, not having a college degree does close certain doors. Compounding the economic effects, that more men are skipping college is bound to widen the cultural gulf between the sexes. And this too has been the experience of black women.

Given the flight of so many men—first black and then white—from family responsibilities, women have had to learn how to support themselves. That this is happening can be seen most vividly in education, especially in preparation for professional fields. The table on the next page compares the ratio of degrees granted to white and black women in 2000 at the undergraduate level and in five professional areas. If white women are still behind men in postgraduate programs, they are drawing close in law and medicine and academic doctorates. Not the least reason some are staying in school may be that today's women realize the odds against maintaining a marriage, so they feel well-advised to have income-producing credentials and skills. Indeed, some have already learned this lesson from their mothers. Black women have long been aware of these probabilities, and hence their investment in professional education. Given their representation among current graduates, by the next generation they will account for a majority of the physicians, lawyers, dentists, and professors of their race.

All indications are that in the coming years, white women will approach the percentages now registered by black women. These days, for every 100 white women graduating from college, there are only 76 white men. We will soon learn whether—or when—they will

EDUCATED AND EMPLOYED

Women's Percentage of Degrees Awarded Within Each Racial Group

	BAs	MBAs	Law
Black Women	65.8%	57.5%	60.7%
White Women	56.7%	38.6%	44.0%

	MDs	Dental	PhDs
Black Women	61.0%	57.0%	61.2%
White Women	40.5%	35.0%	48.2%

Women's Percentage in Workforce Within Each Racial Group

	1970	2000
Black Women	44.3%	53.4%
White Women	37.0%	46.8%

Women's Percentage of Managers and Executives Within Each Racial Group

	1970	2000
Black Women	28.2%	59.5%
White Women	16.2%	44.9%

RACE AND MARRIAGE

Black Women		All Aged 40–44	White Women	
1970	**2000**		**1970**	**2000**
58.3%	40.3%	Currently Married	83.0%	71.4%
33.9%	29.5%	Formerly Married	11.8%	19.9%
7.8%	30.2%	Never Married	5.2%	8.7%
100.0%	100.0%		100.0%	100.0%

reach the current ratio of 100 black women to 52 black men. The likelihood of such a convergence can be seen by looking at the bottom half of the table, which shows the number of working people by race and gender for 1970 and 2000. Black women have gone from 44.3 percent of all black workers to over half. White women are now slightly ahead of where black women were in 1970, and they too may become the majority of their race's workforce during the next few decades. Black women have also jumped from having 28.2 percent of managerial positions held by blacks to more than twice that share. One has only to look at businesses, schools, and government offices to see that most of their black administrators are women. White women held only a small percentage of management jobs in 1970, but by the year 2000, their proportion had almost tripled. Clearly, their education, ambition, and talent led to these promotions. To the extent that affirmative action played a part, they also benefited because employers tended to feel more comfortable with women of either race than black men. (Needless to say, this is never said aloud. Instead, employers state that they would happily hire more black men if they could find some who could fit in as professional and personal colleagues.)

As white women come to match black women's proportions in education and careers, this may also affect their marriage prospects. As the table on this page shows, the share of black women in their early forties who were currently married fell from 58.3 percent in 1970 to 40.3 percent in 2000. This means that by the end of the last century, six in ten were no longer married or had never been married at all. Most striking is the increase in this group, from 7.8 percent to 30.2 percent. The changes among white women were more gradual, but they still show signs of starting to converge with the black distribution. For the present, more white women are marrying, even if fewer of their unions last, but each year the number who don't marry at all is inching up.

INTERRACIAL ROMANCE

Another trend has drained the pool of possible husbands for black women. Interracial marriages are now much more common than in the past, which in some ways is a sign that old barriers are being breached. The 2000 Census located 307,000 such couples, with another 56,000 living together without a license. What is revealing is that in almost three quarters of these households—73.8 percent—the pair included a black man and a white woman. This figure reflects the freedom of black men to find willing partners outside their race, and decisions by white women to live with men they want. What is less clear is why so many fewer white men are drawn to black women. For some, it may be a fear that being known to have a black mate might affect their social standing and career chances. Or it could be that they lack the insight and imagination to look beyond someone's color to find that she is an impressive human being.

Whatever the reason, the fact remains that the number of such interracial couples is small, even less than for Asian and white matches. However, the more numerous pairings of a black man with a white woman can only reduce the pool of black men remaining for black women. So when white women fret about a lack of available men, black women can only agree, and add they've had to deal with this kind of problem for a long time.

11

Pay, Positions, Power:
Inching Toward Equity

The very word *equity* has an appealing ring. Yet its meaning is elusive, provoking disagreements and disputes. All of us have views on the justice or fairness of varied economic arrangements. So when we hear of someone's income, we may find ourselves applauding or shaking our heads or simply gaping in awe. Yet despite having opinions on who should get how much, few of us have fused them into a coherent theory. True, many economists insist that an unfettered market produces the fairest distribution of opportunities and rewards. But most of us can see situations where that doesn't happen, and that's just one example of the elusiveness of equity.

In the United States, as elsewhere, by every economic measure, men rank well ahead of women. To start with the simplest ratio, in 2000, the median income for all men over 25 was $35,842, while the figure for women was $22,887. So women end up with $639 for every $1,000 going to men, after decades of pressure to move closer to parity. (This ratio, which conveys the same information as a percentage, will be used throughout this chapter.)

But note that the $639 figure refers to *income*. This is a broad rubric, combining money from many sources. It includes not only wages and salaries, but also proceeds from inheritances and investments, alimony and pensions, as well as gambling winnings and capital gains. Most significantly, the low median figure for women reflects the fact that many have no income of their own. In the year 2000, a quarter of the 46.6 million married women between the ages of 25 and

64 did not work or receive earnings. Women in this group are not counted as part of the official workforce, even though they put in many hours maintaining a home and rearing children. Needless to say, it isn't possible to agree on how much a homemaker's work is worth. Professional couples looking for a reliable nanny often pay as much as $30,000, plus room and board. Perhaps at-home wives and mothers should receive similar salaries, although proposals along these lines should specify the source of the funding. As for how much, it probably couldn't be higher than the median earnings of women employed at full-time jobs outside their home, which now come to $27,352.

For better or worse, measures of economic equity are based not on all sources of income, but by comparing how much men and women earn by working for outside employers. During 2000, there were 77.0 million men and 68.8 million women who had some kind of paid employment, with the median earnings for women coming to $611 for each $1,000 made by men. This is a considerable disparity, with the women's ratio even lower than for all sources of income. The first reason for the gap is that 39.7 percent of employed women have part-time jobs or work only part of the year, which usually means lower paychecks. (Among employed men, 25.8 percent work part-time or part-year.)

So a more valid comparison, and the one generally used, is to compare the earnings of the 58.7 million men and 41.5 million women who worked at full-time jobs throughout the entire year. When this is done, the women's ratio rises to $733 per each $1,000 going to men. This is still a sizable disparity, and uncovering reasons for it will occupy much of this chapter. Even so, it is an advance over the past, as the table on the next page shows.

At the outset of the 1950s, women tended to be confined to lower-tier occupations, like secretaries and salesclerks, where their wages were less than half those for men. By 1960, changes were obviously under way, since the ratio had risen by $121 during the preceding decade. Yet after that, from 1960 through 1980, the women's ratios barely budged; in fact, they dropped from $607 to $602. By 1990, there had been a considerable rise to $716; but by 2000, their ratio advanced by only seventeen dollars. How can we explain the two quite impressive spurts, followed by periods of leveling off?

FROM PANTRIES TO PAYROLLS

The decade of the 1960s was memorable in many respects, including campus protests, the sexual revolution, and movements toward racial equality. There were also changes in the realm of employment. As can also be seen by looking at the table, the percentage of women working and their share of the workforce did not alter radically. So why did their wage ratio rise from $486 in 1950 to $607 in 1960?

Prior to 1950, domestic traditions prevailed over pocketbook considerations. Husbands said they earned enough and wanted their wives at home, and that largely settled the matter. Or at least it did until the onset of the 1960s. In what seemed like a sudden spurt, millions of women were deciding that they wanted to do more with their lives than be full-time housekeepers and mothers. They were adopting new attitudes and expectations, leading them to a new conception of the person they wanted to be. This was the first stage of a revolution, and its impact has been chronicled in every chapter of this book.

WOMEN AT WORK: CAUSE FOR APPLAUSE?

Percent of Women Who Work	Percent of Women in Workforce		Women's Pay vs. Men's*	Change During Decade
31.4%	29.4%	1950	$486	
				+$121
34.8%	33.3%	1960	$607	
				- $2
42.6%	37.7%	1970	$605	
				- $3
51.5%	42.2%	1980	$602	
				+$114
57.5%	45.4%	1990	$716	
				+$17
63.4%	47.2%	2000	$733	

*Median earnings for women per $1,000 made by men, among year-round full-time workers.

Women were going to work for another reason as well: their families felt they needed a second income. As it happened, most husbands were bringing home decent paychecks, and the majority of households were nowhere near the poverty line. But the 1960s also began to see new waves of enticing consumer products. These included material goods, like the first home air conditioners and color televisions, as well as services like psychotherapy and cosmetic surgery. Plus the greater accessibility of activities such as skiing and foreign travel. As was noted in an earlier chapter, raising children had also become more expensive, since parents were setting higher expectations for them. So second incomes were wanted not because families couldn't make ends meet, but due to having bigger ideas about what a satisfying life ought to include.

And for all those wives to go to work, there had to be jobs available. This was noted at the time by Marvin Harris, an imaginative anthropologist. "It is a great deception to believe that women went out and found jobs," he wrote. On the contrary, "the national economy created vast numbers of jobs that went looking for married women." Moreover, wives were aptly suited for these new positions:

> The great bulk of new jobs were of two types: low-level information-processing jobs such as file-clerks, secretaries, typists, and receptionists; and low-level people-processing jobs such as nurses, primary school teachers, retail sales help, medical and dental assistants, guidance counselors, and social workers.
>
> Her qualifications were superb. She was available in vast numbers. She had been trained for her entire life to be unaggressive and take orders from men. Her husband earned more than she did, so she would take a job that was neither permanent nor secure.

What should be added is that productivity was advancing during the 1960s, mainly because machines were replacing people in blue-collar occupations. Companies used the cash saved from those wages to create new white-collar positions. Tax revenues were also expanding, allowing for more white-collar hirings in the public sector. Nurses and teachers were offered greater salaries than typists and telephone operators had been receiving. Even so, throughout the 1960s and 1970s, women's earnings didn't change much at all, largely because most women were new to the world of work, and settled for support positions with few prospects for promotions. Moreover, the majority did not have college degrees, which limited whatever aspirations they did have. Still, if the arrival of women in the workforce was a major upheaval, few of those who took part in it regarded themselves as revolutionaries.

As it emerged, it was the daughters of typists and teachers and stay-at-home mothers who were starting to see themselves in a new light. Most significantly, they were aspiring to careers that previously had been the preserves of men. In those ten years, the number of medical degrees awarded to women rose from 8.4 percent to 23.4 percent; while in dentistry, they went from 0.9 percent to 13.3 percent. And in the law schools, the number of degrees earned by women increased by a factor of five, from 5.4 percent to 30.2 percent. Having qualified in professions where men set the standards and compensation, more women were starting with salaries identical or very close to men's. Not only that, they were postponing getting married and having children, first to further graduate education, and then to gain a foothold in their careers. As a result, during the 1980 to 1990 decade, women were attaining the seniority and experience that bring higher earnings.

The table on the next page highlights occupational changes over the past 30 years, showing how women have been joining—and often replacing—men in a broad array of jobs, ranging from insurance adjusters and pharmacists to dentists and bartenders. Still, titles can be deceptive. Insurance adjusters were once mainly men who went out and inspected damaged cars. Today, most of them are women, who sit at computers filing claims. In other occupations, like medicine under managed care, women are entering when the profession is changing. This is one reason why their earnings ratio moved only from $716 to $733 between 1990 and 2000.

Another inescapable fact is that in almost every occupation they have entered, from neurosurgery to investment banking, at mid-career women still have not advanced as far as men. Thus at Deloitte & Touche, one of the largest accounting firms, women comprise half of the young people they hire every year, all of whom are paid on the same scale. However, not long thereafter, the women begin to fall

WOMEN'S SHARES WITHIN OCCUPATIONS

	1970	2001
Total Workforce	37.7%	46.6%

Considerable Change

	1970	2001
Insurance Adjusters	29.6%	72.1%
Educational Administrators	27.8%	64.1%
Publicists	26.6%	60.2%
Government Administrators	21.7%	51.5%
Bartenders	21.0%	50.9%
Pharmacists	12.1%	48.1%
College Faculty	28.6%	43.3%
Veterinarians	5.2%	39.4%
Lawyers	4.9%	29.3%
Physicians	9.7%	29.3%
Architects	4.0%	23.5%
Dentists	3.5%	19.9%
Clergy	2.9%	15.1%
Police Officers	3.7%	14.1%
Telephone Installers	2.8%	13.8%
Engineers	1.7%	10.4%
Sheet Metal Workers	1.9%	5.6%

Essentially No Change

	1970	2001
Secretaries	97.8%	98.4%
Dental Hygienists	94.0%	97.8%
Registered Nurses	97.3%	93.1%
Librarians	82.1%	85.7%
Elementary Teachers	83.9%	82.5%
Computer Programmers	24.2%	26.6%

Men Replacing Women

	1970	2001
Telephone Operators	94.0%	83.3%
Flight Attendants	95.9%	80.5%
Waiters & Waitresses	90.8%	76.4%
Cooks & Chefs	67.2%	42.5%

away. Some depart for family reasons, like deciding to stay at home with young children or accompanying a husband who has been transferred. But more depart because they sense they won't have much of a future with the firm. And they may be right, because when promotions to partner are announced, a typical year sees only one in five going to a woman. So while the women were hired as putative equals, for most that promise is not fulfilled.

STAYING ON THE JOB

Much is made of the fact that men are more likely to have a continuous work record, and most of us agree that experience is important. After all, who wants to be a surgeon's first patient? Unfortunately, no agency tracks the complete work histories of women and men. So among individuals who are currently employed, it isn't possible to say how many have worked without a break after leaving high school or college. However, there is one piece of information we do have. Since 1983, the Bureau of Labor Statistics has tracked how long workers have been with their current employer, which provides some idea about their commitment to work.

The most informative findings are from workers aged 45 to 54, because many in this group are still likely to have children at home, so the women who work will be juggling that responsibility as well. For those in their fifties, the children may have already gone, but they probably lived at home until fairly recently. The next table following this page shows the median years men and women workers have been with their current employer, and how many have been there for ten or more years. As can be seen, the women's median increased slightly between 1983 and 2000. However, the number with ten or more years of service grew from 37.8 percent to 43.6 percent, which is quite close to the proportion of men with that employment record.

What is even more notable is what happened with the men in this age group. Their median figure actually fell, from 12.8 years to 9.5 years, while the number who have worked at the same job for ten years dropped from 60.1 percent to 50.3 percent. Nor is downsizing the primary cause of the men's attrition, since women have also been affected by cutbacks. These findings show, quite clearly, that growing numbers of women are building work experience that should qualify them for promotions. Therefore, it's reasonable to assume that women are not only joining men in the workforce, but are in many cases replacing them.

Social Security provides additional evidence of when men are leaving the workforce. Its rules allow individuals to retire and begin to draw pensions at the age of 62 rather than 65, although starting earlier means your checks will be smaller for the rest of your life. In 1965, less than a third—31.7 percent—of all retiring men asked for their pensions before they were 65. Today, more than twice as many do. In 1999, the most recent year for which figures are available, 69.4 percent of the men were opting to retire early.

Why are so many more men leaving work in their early sixties? Let's acknowledge that some have been let go and feel too old to embark on a new job search. Still others have private pensions or sufficient investments so that they can afford to stop working. But these two groups are not large enough to account for the substantial shift to early retirement. Closer to the truth is that by the age of 62, most men no longer like their jobs. Nor is this only the case for blue-collar workers whose employment is physically wearing. Physicians are stepping down due to the constraints of managed care, as are professors who have ceased enjoying teaching. Also, not everyone in competitive careers makes it to the top. As they grow older, more and more managers find they are being passed over for promotions and must work under executives younger than themselves, some of whom are women. Perhaps in the past, men didn't like their work either. Even so, in 1970, of those between the ages of 60 and 64, 70.6 percent were showing up at their jobs. By 2000, those who were still at work had dropped to 54.5 percent.

COMPARABLE PAY
FOR COMPARABLE PERFORMANCE?

In the economic arena, equity means giving everyone a chance to show their talents and linking rewards to performance. To be sure, this is the ideal, and not yet a reality. Aptitudes often go undiscovered, due to prejudice or lack of encouragement. Even with these barriers, women as a group are coming closer to having an equal opportunity in embarking on careers. As has been noted, they either outnumber men or are approaching them in gaining the academic credentials required by many occupations.

The next issue is whether these gains will be followed by advancement up the career ladder. At present, there isn't much evidence that this is happening. A rough gauge of recognition is how much people are paid. Of course, there are many reasons for disparities in earnings. Therefore, the table on the next page confines itself to comparable women and men employed at full-time jobs for the entire year, thus excluding part-time workers with lower earnings. Their ages have also been made as similar as possible: persons 35 to 44 in the first section, and 25 to 44 in the second, which are the ranges the Census uses.

The top part of the table shows the earnings of men and women workers with bachelor's degrees. As their ages are 35 to 44, it seems safe to assume that most of the women are mothers. Even so, they have shown a serious commitment to work by pursuing full-time

STICKING TO THE JOB: WORKERS AGED 45–54

Median Years with Current Employer

Men		Women	
1983	2000	1983	2000
12.8	9.5	6.3	7.3

Ten or More Years at Current Employer

Men		Women	
1983	2000	1983	2000
60.1%	50.3%	37.8%	43.6%

MATCHING WOMEN AND MEN

Bachelor's (College)

3,659,000 men and 2,399,000 women: all of whom have bachelor's degrees, are between 35 and 44, and were employed full-time throughout the year in 2000.

	Men	Women
Over $100,000	16.1%	3.8%
$75,000–$100,000	14.5%	7.0%
$50,000–$75,000	30.3%	23.7%
Under $50,000	39.1%	65.5%
	100.0%	100.0%
Median Income	$57,079	$41,136

Bachelor's (Marital)

8,012,000 men and 5,476,000 women: all of whom have never married, are between 25 and 44, and worked full-time throughout the year during 2000.

	Men	Women
Over $100,000	3.2%	1.9%
$75,000–$100,000	5.3%	3.6%
$50,000–$75,000	13.8%	10.5%
Under $50,000	77.7%	84.0%
	100.0%	100.0%
Median Income	$30,875	$29,086

schedules. Yet despite this avowal and having invested equally in education, the women's median income was $41,136 compared with the men's $57,079, or a ratio of $721 to the men's $1,000. The chief reason for the gap is that fewer women reach the higher earnings levels. Only 34.5 percent of them make over $50,000, compared with 60.9 percent of the men. Figures such as these support the belief that even educated and dedicated women still find they hit a ceiling. Recall the earlier statistics about the accounting firm, where women made up half of the entrants, but only 20 percent of the group who were elevated to partner.

Perhaps this part of the table fails to show whether the two sexes have comparable work records, since there are women who take time off when their children are young, or who may not give their all to the job, due to the pressure of family obligations. So the second part of the table seeks to address this issue by confining itself to full-time workers who have never been married. True, some may have children at home, but not enough to affect the overall analysis.

All of the 5,476,000 women shown here have not married, by choice or circumstance, and are able to give their work all the hours and energy expected by employers. As can be seen, the median earnings of these women yield a ratio of $942, which is closer to men's than any we have seen. While these women still meet a ceiling, the sexual bias isn't as sharp: 5.5 percent of them make $75,000 or more, against 8.5 percent of the men.

ROOM AT THE TOP?

Over the past half century, inordinate power has passed to the chief executives of America's corporations. Each day, these individuals preside over decisions that shape the society and affect the lives of all residents of this country and many abroad. While they may be removed by boards of directors, they are given enormous leeway. After all, they were chosen to put their mark on a company. Each year, *Fortune* magazine lists the country's 1,000 largest firms, ranked by their annual revenues. The roster for 2002 began with Wal-Mart Stores, which took in almost $220 billion and had some 1.4 million employees, and ended with a firm called PC Connection, with revenues of $1.2 billion and 1,312 persons on its payroll. Of the 1,000 CEOs in these companies, eight were women, a representation amounting to less than 1 percent. Let's look at how these eight got to the top.

Six of them rose on corporate ladders, showing talent for leadership early in their careers. Carleton Fiorina, who heads Hewlett-Packard (28th in the top 1,000), was recruited from Lucent Technologies. Patricia Russo, also at Lucent (76th), Anne Mulcahy with Xerox (120th), and Andrea Jung of Avon Products (302nd) were chosen after long careers within their companies. Cinda Hallman of Spherion (539th) had previously been with Conoco and Du Pont, while Dorrit Bern came to Charming Shoppes (987th) after many years at Sears.

The two others took an entrepreneurial path. Patricia Gallup founded PC Connection (1,000th) and presided over its ascent to the top tier. Marion Sandler, working with her husband, put together Golden West Financial (371st) through a series of mergers. They are joint CEOs, and she and her husband assume the title in alternate years.

It's worth noting that only two of the eight preside over firms that cater chiefly to their own sex. Avon, of course, is the home sales company that features cosmetics. Charming Shoppes is a women's clothing chain, with subsidiaries called Fashion Bug and Added Dimension.

Several other women have had the title of chairman; however, they were not CEOs, but rather managed divisions within larger enterprises. This was the case with Stacey Snider of Universal Pictures and Sherry Lansing at Paramount. Or Charlotte Bears and Shelly Lazarus, both of whom led the Ogilvy & Mather advertising agency, which is a subsidiary of a British conglomerate. So the stark fact is that among America's 1,000 largest corporations, more than 99 percent continue to pick men as their top officer. Nor are there signs that this ratio will be changing by more than one or two points in the generation ahead. Indeed, in reviewing the tiers of managers from which the next crop of 1,000 chief executives will be chosen, it isn't easy to identify women who would be leading candidates.

A quite different picture emerges when we look at the Ivy League schools, where three of the eight presidents are women. Duke also has a woman president, as had the University of Chicago. So if women can head billion-dollar enterprises like Princeton and the University of Pennsylvania, why not General Motors or Merrill Lynch? The most common response is to refer to what is called the "pipeline problem." According to this theory, very few women were embarking on corporate careers three decades ago, so only a very small number have enough experience to be considered as current candidates for the top jobs.

In fact, the number of women entering the pipeline in the past was not insignificant. Students who received an MBA in 1975 at about the age of 27 would be 54 in 2002, the approximate age when executives are seen as ready for the ultimate promotion. There is no denying that in 1975, only 8.4 percent of MBAs were awarded to women. Still, that figure isn't zero. That class of 1975 formed a pool of 3,063 women who had committed themselves to business careers, at a time when they weren't sure how welcome they would be. Of course, we know that not all MBAs end up with the largest corporations. Nor, for that matter, is that degree necessary to become a CEO. But simply to pursue a point, let's assume all of these women had entered and stayed in the corporate pipeline. And let's also suppose they possessed the same talents and commitments as their male colleagues. Had these and other conditions been equal and equitable—which they obviously weren't—their original 8.4 percent share would have won them 84 of the 1,000 chairmanships rather than the eight they now have.

EMPIRES OF THEIR OWN

Rivaling *Fortune*'s list of the 1,000 largest firms is *Forbes* magazine's roster of America's 400 wealthiest individuals. The 2001 list began with Bill Gates (at that time, worth some $54 billion) and ended with ten persons with assets of a mere $600 million. Altogether, there were 358 men and 42 women. Among the men, 27 had inherited their money. Some were from such well-known families as the Hearsts and Rockefellers; others' fortunes were more recent, as from Wal-Mart Stores, Getty oil, and Lauder cosmetics. The remaining 331 men were generally self-made, or largely so. Ted Turner and Rupert Murdoch, for example, may have started out with silver spoons, but their own talents transformed them into platinum.

Of the 42 women on the list, 33 inherited their wealth. Few were from historic families; most were widows or daughters of men who made their money in the last half-century, such as Joan Kroc, whose husband founded McDonald's, and Elizabeth Reid of the Hallmark Card family. Another three women might be called *"working heirs."* Abigail Johnson of Fidelity Investments heads the firm founded by her grandfather; Maggie Magerko serves as president of her father's timber company; and Leona Helmsley now runs the real estate empire her late husband built.

This leaves six women who amassed some of America's greatest fortunes, partially or wholly on their own. Doris Fisher opened the first Gap store with her husband in 1969, and the chain has prospered under their dual leadership. Donna Dubinsky became wealthy by being a cofounder of PalmPilot; Theresa Pam pioneered in fiber optics; and Margaret Whitman started eBay, the on-line auction bazaar. The other two women on the *Forbes* list have long been nationally known: Martha Stewart and Oprah Winfrey.

Six out of 400 is slightly better than eight in 1,000, which suggests that women may have more opportunities to prosper as entrepreneurs than inside corporate structures. The successes of Stewart, Winfrey, and Whitman show that women, as much as men, have the talent and temperament to create things that people come to want. There was no "demand" for Stewart's sense of style or Winfrey's personalized programming or Whitman's on-line auction. But it turns out that these were products that tens of millions of consumers felt they had to have, even if they did not realize it until they were made available.

ENTERING MASCULINE TERRAIN

Women have certainly shown that they are not dissuaded by competition. Each year, they enter the college application arena, where they vie with men for coveted places at schools like UCLA and Stanford, and later to obtain a law degree from Harvard or study medicine at Cornell. The year 2000 found that 959 colleges had women's basketball teams, 778 sponsored softball, and 724 played soccer against other schools. There can be no doubt that the women who play on these teams want to win and work rigorously to attain that goal. And in another sphere, beauty pageants are still part of the American scene, and a lot of effort and ambition are invested in vying for those crowns.

Yet something happens after those early successes. Of the 1975 MBA graduates, the majority may not be at-home housewives, but not more than a handful rose to levels achieved by men in their class. Indeed, signs of their falling away are evident every day. In 2002, Morgan Stanley listed its 153 new managing directors, of whom 17 were women. A 2001 *National Law Journal* study of 250 leading firms found that women comprised 30.3 percent of their lawyers, but were 15.7 percent of the partners, and most of them were recent appointments.

Much has been said and written about why fewer women stay the course. While many reasons can be cited, two are on every list and deserve close attention. One may be considered *cultural,* and the other is *personal,* although they are related and overlap.

While no one says so explicitly, most of the nation's major institutions have a masculine culture. Can an organization have a gender? Of course, so long as we acknowledge how the term is being used. Few doubt that the National Football League has a masculine identity, even though some women are avid fans. The U.S. Naval Academy is officially coeducational, and 16 percent of its current enrollment are women. Yet they go there knowing it is a man's world; indeed, all its students are still referred to as *midshipmen.* In civilian life, women students quickly sense the masculine character of Yale University and Stanford Medical School, even when they comprise half of the enrollments, since they face legacies entrenched by long duration.

Where businesses are concerned, a taste for competition is not enough; the ultimate aim is *conquest.* America's economic history is littered with once-dominant firms that failed to rise to new challenges, or maintain their market share, or retain the confidence of investors. If a company begins to fall behind, the vultures start circling. True, some revive after a spell on the critical list; but a more likely fate for the company is to be merged or acquired and lose its identity. This is the setting in which executives are expected to commit their loyalty and energy. Men have long been raised to accept these demands. Until recently, few women had role models or mentors to guide them along this path for a fulfilling life.

Nor is business the only arena where participants are judged by the bottom line. In law firms, for example, technical skill is not enough. Your work must also become widely recognized, so your reputation brings in new clients. Of course, being personable may help, as can a flair for self-promotion. Similar conditions prevail in medicine, whose epicenters are the teaching hospitals. Here too professional proficiency does not suffice. Physicians are also expected to attain a reputation that will attract a flow of fee-paying patients. Alternately, they may be judged on the research grants they receive. And academe is no longer an ivory tower. Faculty members know they must produce publications that gain them renown in their discipline. This must be done early to gain tenure, and later to attract offers from other institutions. Faculty members who don't do research will find they are assessed on how many students they attract, as deans have printouts showing which teachers are pulling their weight.

The point of course is that women as well as men are being held to these standards. In all fields, also, new employees know they are competing against others at their level—with whom they work on a daily basis—for a limited number of promotions. The culture of competition thus operates on two fronts. First, as has been noted, it calls for vying against colleagues for rewards and recognition. More than that, it demands giving your all to the organization as it seeks to surpass others in the field. On the whole, men are more receptive to this regimen than women, in part because they have been raised to be more comfortable with the notion of competition. In addition, they may take more readily to long working hours, not least because the office becomes their "club," with a camaraderie familiar to their sex. (It probably doesn't hurt that if they do have families, the chances are that Mom is either at home taking care of the children, or will be arriving earlier to relieve the baby-sitter.)

This is not to say that law firms and investment banks are fraternity houses writ large. But there are times when that analogy is not entirely misplaced. For example, corporations often buy season tickets to sporting events for entertaining clients. True, women executives are now asked to join the group. But also expected is an ability to banter about a sport, which requires a savviness that many men begin picking up before the age of ten. Then there's golf with clients and colleagues. Of course, women can be expert on the links and keep up with most men. Even so, those who pick high-powered careers are not usually as fixated on this pastime, which can cut them out of a fellowship where connections are made. (Nor are all men pleased to have women join them on the course.) And even women who have these skills find that it is the showers and locker-rooms where formalities are dropped and bonding occurs. So long as this culture predominates, women will continually have to prove themselves in this basically masculine domain. Some do, very impressively; but it takes a lot of extra effort.

HOME AND FAMILY SECOND?

The personal factor centers on the demands of being a spouse and a parent, which generally loom larger in the lives of women. Even today, a wife's career can strain a marriage, since there are still some husbands who can't adjust to their wife's commitments outside the home. This happened with Ann Landers, the advice columnist, and Ellen Fein, a coauthor of *The Rules,* both of whose husbands initiated divorces because they felt they weren't getting the attention they deserved. A further test comes when a wife's career advancement involves a transfer or accepting a job offer in a new location. Despite notable exceptions, not many husbands have been willing to give up, say, their medical practice in Boston to move with her to San Diego. Here the marriage may be at stake, and to ensure its survival, she is more likely to be the one who steps off the fast track. If nothing else, she is not unaware of a statistic cited in an earlier chapter: the rising ratio of unattached women who now work alongside men like her husband.

One solution to the work-vs.-family dilemma was found by Carleton Fiorina at Hewlett-Packard, Anne Mulcahy at Xerox, and other executives at or near the top at Oracle, Pitney Bowes, and Exodus Communications. All of their husbands are retired, which usually means they are older, and their own careers peaked earlier. Some of these women are second wives, and were in their late thirties when they married. Because of the pressures they faced during their corporate climbs, most of them haven't had children.

While the Census doesn't report how many successful women become mothers, it does tell us the marital status of those with high earnings. As was seen in the chapter on the double standard, among the Americans who make more than $100,000, the men were much more likely to be in intact marriages. Twice as many of the women had never been married, and they were almost four times more likely to have once been married but no longer are. Several explanations were suggested. One is that men are made uneasy by successful women, and so choose dates and mates they find less threatening. Another is that many of these women may set exacting standards, and have not found men who satisfy them. Or perhaps they just haven't found the time or occasions to meet potential partners.

"All women," Sylvia Ann Hewlett once wrote, "yearn to have children." This is obviously an exaggeration. (Unless one wants to argue that even women who deny they do actually want to become mothers have repressed that desire.) Still, it seems clear that most women would like to bear a child, and most of them will, even if the number will be smaller than in the past. At the same time, more women are preparing for professions where too much attention to children might impede their careers. Catalyst, an organization that studies women in the workplace, actually went out and spoke with financial executives in their forties who had worked continuously. Half of them had never had children.

We can agree that pursuing a successful career makes exacting demands. Not uncommonly, rising within an organization or building a business or a profession becomes a prime priority, often superceding family obligations and a social life. As is also well known, many men choose this route, despite laments from their wives and the dismay of their children. Hence a question that is commonly heard: How many women actually desire to ascend on that track, especially if there are strong odds of their ending up single or childless or otherwise on their own? As matters now stand, more than a few are deciding to step off after promising starts, due to seventy-hour weeks and having work on their mind the rest of the time. This noted, the fact remains that increasing numbers of women are making clear that they aspire to such careers, well aware of the sacrifices they may have to make. They can already be seen rising in the military and college administrations, in fields like journalism and advertising, as well as serving as judges and elected officials. So the point is to take seriously women who are in it for the long haul, even if they are not at first readily distinguishable from others with less certain commitments. After all, the signs are that there are going to be fewer men with the qualities and competence expected at the top.

THE WAY WE LIVE NOW

Women have more choices than ever before; but they also face new conflicts and constraints. While no single trend is enveloping all women, some attitudes and aspirations have become widespread. In this regard, the Census sheds light on decisions millions of women have been making, in particular, by showing the settings in which they are exploring their options. This is illustrated by information con-

HOW MANY MOTHERS WORK?

Married Women with Children Under Six Whose Husbands Work Full-time

	Wife's Work Status		
Family Income	Works Full-time (3,586,000)	Works Part-time (3,407,000)	Does Not Work (3,318,000)
Over $100,000	23.6%	18.4%	16.8%
$50,000–$100,000	52.1%	45.2%	32.4%
Under $50,000	24.3%	36.4%	50.8%
	100.0%	100.0%	100.0%
Median Income	$68,906	$60,459	$48,834

cerning 10,311,000 women who had these attributes: first, they were married; second, their husband had a full-time year-round job; third, they had at least one child under the age of six. The Census also tells us that fully employed husbands generally have higher earnings than other men. So what did these mothers do?

As it turned out, the 10,311,000 women fell into three groups of almost-equal size. One group, which was the largest by a small margin, consisted of mothers who took full-time jobs outside their homes. In another, the smallest, all the mothers stayed at home. And in the third, the mothers worked part-time.

The table on the previous page does not tell how much the working mothers made, since that is not our concern here. Rather, it shows the effect their employment had on their households. Let's start with the mothers who spent full-time at home, which we may presume was their choice. As can be seen, half of them have husbands who make over $50,000, so it could be argued that in those homes his income could handle the family bills. (And that would certainly be so with the 16.8 percent who earn over $100,000, since if they have one child under six, it is unlikely others are in college.) But equally interesting is that in half of these families, the husband earned less than $50,000, which must mean that some made considerably less than that. Yet these couples still seem to feel that the mother's being at home is preferable to her working, even though the extra cash might help. These 3,318,000 families are a significant group, and their decisions deserve attention.

For a woman to take a full-time job when she has a child under six can be an elaborate undertaking. So before examining their decisions, it would be well to recall that it isn't always easy to arrange at-home or outside care for children who are under six, not to mention recurrent anxieties over whether all is going well. A central question is how far these families really *need* a second paycheck. That is undoubtedly the case with the 24.3 percent whose joint earnings total less than $50,000, and it is probably so for those at the lower reaches of the $50,000 to $100,000 range. But for most homes where both spouses are fully employed, it is more likely that two incomes elevate their living standard to an *upper*-middle-class level.

The remaining 3,407,000 wives are significant in showing that while two thirds of young mothers now work, almost half of them have intermittent employment. This in turn suggests that the home-to-work revolution is not yet complete and may never be. As the table shows, wives who hold part-time jobs help to give their families a median income of $60,459, which is $11,625 more than those where only the husband works. These additions make a difference to family budgets, but they aren't really enough to move a household from one class to another.

Not all women aspire to becoming heads of corporations any more than all men do. Still, women who do have these and similar ambitions want a fair chance to have their talents rewarded and recognized, which is what men have always sought. But equity may be even more important elsewhere on the economic scale. The 2000 Census counted 9,681,000 single women who had children aged seventeen or younger, and most of these mothers now must work full-time to support their families. As was shown in an earlier chapter, over 80 percent of them earn less than $35,000, so they are much more likely to be waitresses or checkout clerks than to hold professional positions. Whether these women are single by choice or circumstance, they are a growing group and are raising an increasing proportion of the nation's children. By any moral measure, improving their economic status should have the highest priority.

12

The Pairing Problem

History, properly construed, is more than a chronicle of the past. On a broader canvas, it is a conjunction of forces that created the world we know and is shaping its future form. While history is made by human beings, so many take part in the process that trends take on lives of their own, often catching us unaware and unprepared. For example, no concerted campaigns led to the increased reliance on contraception and abortion and divorce. However, we find ourselves living with all three, and decisions that have been made regarding them have brought changes that earlier generations would never have imagined.

SEX AND POLITICS: A DEEPENING DIVIDE

In theory, two people can have divergent political opinions and still live amiably together. We can all cite households where one partner is conservative and the other leans to the left. Yet on further reflection, we would probably have to confess that we can't think of more than one or two such pairings. The reason is that most positions on issues are not just about a specific subject, but reflect broader moral and ideological principles. And these tenets in turn express much about the person we are; say, what we feel we owe the world and what our own entitlements are. So it isn't easy to visualize a determined right-to-life proponent sharing bed and breakfast with someone who wants abortions to be readily available.

In chapter 7 on masculinity, figures were given showing marked differences between the genders on gun control and military spending. To make a point, let's imagine that all the women who favor greater curbs on guns and less reliance on missiles would prefer to find a man who shares their views. On first hearing, this may seem like a reasonable request. The problem is that there aren't enough agreeable men to go around. For every 100 women who take a dim view of home arsenals, there are only 69 men who hold similar views. On the missile issue, only 59 men have matching opinions.

In the 2000 election, a CBS–New York Times survey found that among unmarried voters, 63 percent of the women cast their ballots for Albert Gore, while only 48 percent of the single men did. Given the shortfall of Gore men, and since fewer men voted, the odds were that only 64 women in 100 would find a fellow political spirit. And the imbalance is actually greater, since some of the men who supported Gore are gay. However, among the Bush singles, the men would have to do some searching, since for every 100 of them, there were only 82 women.

MARRIAGE MATERIAL?

Traditionally, the chief measure of a man's being seen as marriageable was whether he made enough to support a family, or had prospects for doing so. It used to be that the prospective bride's father quizzed his daughter's beau on how much he earned and where his career was headed. Of course, that was in a distant past. Still, as chapter 6 on the double standard noted, old ideas often persist in new guises.

Simply for the sake of argument, let's grant that even today, there are *some* women who would like to have a husband who earns more than they do. It need not be by much: fewer women now set their sights on having a *rich husband,* which was once a standard story line. Moreover, her reasons need not be monetary: she may feel her husband would be happier in the marriage if his paycheck was somewhat larger. On a more practical level, his earnings may have to suffice, in the event that she wants to take off time from her job after the birth of a baby.

The 2000 Census has some figures that illuminate this subject. As an exercise, we can compare two sets of individuals who aren't married, or are divorced and haven't remarried. The first group consists of single women who currently earn between $40,000 and $50,000. The second contains all the unattached men who make from $50,000 to $60,000. If these women and men were to pair off, the women would all end up with mates averaging $10,000 more than they made. The Census tabulations show that if the sexes are lined up this way, there are only 80 available men for every 100 women with incomes just below theirs. (The ratios are similar when other ranges are used.) And, as was recalled earlier, some of those 80 men will be gay, while fewer of the 100 women will identify as lesbian.

One reason for the imbalance is that more women are now at the $40,000 to $50,000 level, well ahead of what secretaries and receptionists used to make. While the chapter on economic equity made clear that men overall have higher earnings, a critical mass of women is emerging who make as much as men and sometimes more. As a result, many women will find themselves having to ask if they want to settle down with men who bring home less than they do.

A CULTURE GAP

A statistic cited in several chapters is that 57.2 percent of bachelor's degrees are now awarded to women, which works out to 75 men completing college for every 100 women. As the chapter on education argued, women seem more suited to the academic regimen. The chapter also emphasized that individuals can show intelligence—not to mention brilliance—in many different ways. So it stands to reason that there are equal numbers of smart people in both sexes, even if their aptitudes are sometimes in different spheres.

It is a commonplace that pairings work best if there are some shared interests. Needless to say, this doesn't have to be across the board. She doesn't have to cheer with him at football games, nor need he join her when she searches for an exotic olive oil. Indeed, it makes sense to have time and pastimes apart from one another. This acknowledged, let's imagine a situation where the wife is a college graduate, while the husband learned a trade and now owns a plumbing business.

For the next three Sunday nights she wants to watch a television adaptation of a Henry James novel. To say that he doesn't share this interest is an understatement. Well, yes, a lot of homes have several sets, so he could repair to the den and select another channel. Or she might arrange to watch with some women friends, while he goes out with the guys.

But it is important to her that they watch *The Golden Bowl* together, kindled by her hope that afterward they will exchange their thoughts about it. In her view, they've not been sharing enough of their lives, and she feels she's owed his willingness to join in an activity of her choosing. To be sure, the fact that he didn't go to college isn't the entire problem. There are men with graduate degrees who find Henry James soporific, just as there are self-made men who become serious connoisseurs. Even so, the college gap is accentuating a cultural divide. (Even women who major in, say, accounting, are affected by the liberal arts ambience of a campus.)

Or look at the visitors in an art museum. On weekdays, most will be women by themselves or in pairs. On weekends, when there are more couples, many of the men seem to be there under duress, glancing furtively at their watches and wondering if they are nearing the exit. Doubtless this was ever so. What is different today is that women want more from their mates and expect those goals to be realized. Simply stated, the sexual gulf is greater because sights are being set higher.

Recall the chapter in which it was asked why women were more apt to initiate divorces. As was seen, husbands can be quite satisfied with a marriage that their wives find deficient. Part of the mismatch is that the man's needs are simpler, with many of them physical. This includes not just sex, but also having a fully furnished home, food on hand and meals prepared, and clothes ready for wearing. He also expects emotional support, including cheers for his triumphs and commiseration for setbacks. Modern men aren't like their fathers in that they are less likely to hide themselves behind a newspaper. But there are still some who try to avoid being drawn into conversations they regard as rambling or having no practical point. Like being asked to analyze the bond between Adam and Maggie Verver in *The Golden Bowl*.

WOMEN JUDGE MEN; MEN JUDGE WOMEN

Let's pinpoint another specific group: women in their thirties who are not currently married. In 2000, there were 7.4 million women in this group, amounting to 35.0 percent of those that age, the largest unmarried quotient in the nation's history. In earlier generations, almost all women this age had married young and were still wed to their only husband. And that meant their experience of life was more limited. Their current counterparts have had more opportunity to learn how the world works; in particular, they have come to know men, often quite a few of them. While most of these women are not averse to marriage or a sustained relationship—for the first time or again—they are not sanguine about its chances of success.

Women are now more openly judgmental about men, and with more of a cutting edge, than ever in the past, especially in the age range just cited. (Epithets like *jerk, creep,* and *loser* often crop up in accounts of dates that didn't work out.) In their view, these men simply aren't interesting or intelligent enough to be considered serious companions. All too often, first encounters matter in the dating and mating game. A usual overture is for him to say something he thinks is witty, to show that he is a clever fellow. In the past, girls would laugh obligingly at his unfunny jokes. Such indulgence is less evident today: women are more apt to respond with a chilly stare.

In fact, let's go back to the past. Almost a century ago, in 1910, the graduating classes of New York City's high schools totaled 1,514 girls and 963 boys. In those days, the girls who finished high school eventually became teachers or might work up to being office managers. The many boys who left school early became butchers and construction workers. Yet the 1910 Census also shows that schoolteachers were willing to marry welders, even if they weren't strong on conversation. A woman counted herself fortunate if she could say "he's a good provider," and add that "he cares about the children."

Another, more recent, set of figures further illuminates this perspective. In 1998, the Census compared the educational levels of the nation's married couples. (It no longer publishes these data.) The format made it possible to isolate couples where the husband was forty-five or older, which means they got married about 1975 or earlier. With the white couples, the husband was 52.4 percent more likely to have had more education than his wife. That was customary in that generation, since before 1980, men outnumbered women among college graduates. But among the blacks in the Census study, it was the wives who had more schooling, by an edge of 62.8 percent. And these marriages seemed to work despite the disparity, since divorces were less common than they are today. Chapter 10 on race wondered whether the experience of black Americans has omens for white families. Given the gap in college degrees among white women and men, it will be interesting to see whether the women will follow the model found in many black households, and marry men with less formal education. And that, of course, takes us back to affinities for Henry James.

MARTY: MORE THAN A MOVIE

Despite the abundance of ratios favoring men that have been cited in this book, it is striking how many of them can be heard complaining that they are unable to meet women. Yet in any metropolitan area, bookstores, gyms, and galleries show no shortage of unattached women willing—if suitably approached—to open a conversation. Not to mention the ubiquitous bars and personals and dating services, as well as religious groups and cultural gatherings. So what's the problem for these men? Some will be candid enough to admit that they encounter the "get lost" look when they try to make an overture. But the remedy is not a new opening line. The obstacle lies elsewhere, and it's one the men seldom admit. It was poignantly depicted back in 1955, in the year's Oscar-winning movie called *Marty*. Its hero was a Bronx butcher, who never made it with girls. In the opening scenes, we saw him and his friends evaluating women, replete with sneers for those they called *dogs,* referring to women they wouldn't be seen with, even if the men were no bargains themselves.

Five decades have passed, and things have hardly changed for men who aren't particularly charming or clever. Let's say, on a scale of ten, we're talking about men who are a two or a three themselves, which they probably realize, but would rather not think about. Their problems arise because they consider themselves superior to women who have the same rankings they do.(Let's agree that labeling people as twos or threes or tens is invidious and unfair; but in the world we know, first impressions often count.) So they confine their approaches to women who are seen as more attractive. However, those women are apt to have better options, so the men's overtures tend to be rebuffed.

So here we have yet another mismatch, which leaves a lot of loose ends. Men pursue prizes beyond their grasp, when they could be perfectly content with someone who isn't viewed as a great catch. So these men lose, not only by failing to get what they covet but also in the chance for a happy ending. As you will have guessed, in *Marty* the hero falls in love with a woman he had earlier dismissed, with some affecting scenes where he tries to conceal the attachment from his friends.

PUBLIC POLICIES AND PRIVATE LIVES

American ideology stresses self-reliance and the right to pursue happiness in ways of our own choosing. As a result, we believe that government should only intrude if a case can be convincingly made. Of course, where emotions and interests are involved, consistency cannot always be expected. Liberals generally defend freedoms of expression and are opposed to censorship. But they want firmer controls over what they regard as business excesses. For their part, conservatives cherish the right to own firearms, drive heavyweight vehicles, and pay a bare minimum in taxes. So it is noteworthy that many of them are now advocating measures aimed at exposing what the sexes do in private to public attention.

As was noted earlier, several states have created a covenant form of marriage, which would be more difficult to dissolve. On the national level, Congress created a competition among the states, with monetary rewards going to those reducing their out-of-wedlock births. In 2002, the Speaker of the House of Representatives proposed allocating $100 million in federal funds annually for "premarital marriage education and divorce reduction programs." While marriage and divorce are still in individuals' hands, conservatives hope the power and influence of government will change the ways people think about these decisions. In fact, counseling can help a strained relationship when both spouses want to keep their marriage going, and an outside party provides insights and advice. But sessions prior to marriage are mainly verbal exercises about a reality that has yet to occur. The two people may be asked what they want from the marriage, and potential differences will be discussed. Or possible conflicts will be cited, with each asked how they might address them. Every so often, the two will hear enough from each other to decide to call the wedding off, and that at least forestalls a divorce. But there is no firm evidence that pointers offered before a marriage have much effect once the sharing of actual beds and bathrooms gets under way

A more elemental intervention involves attempts to reduce early sexual activity. The most obvious targets are teenagers, whose rates of intercourse, pregnancy, and births have alarmed many adults. A 1995 study by the Department of Health and Human Services found that 22.1 percent of fifteen-year-old girls had already started having sex. From sixteen through eighteen, the figures rose successively to 38.0 percent, 51.1 percent, and 65.4 percent. (The double standard apparently affects social science, since these surveys seldom ask young men about their initiation.)

In 1996, the Congress responded by enacting its Abstinence Education Program, offering $87.5 million annually to states for creating courses that would teach sexual restraint. Within four years, 36 states had started such instruction, of which 27 made abstention the only option, which meant the curriculum couldn't even mention contraception or abortion. In New York, one program was called *Not Me, Not Now.* Ohio had an *Operation Keepsake;* in Utah it was *Teen Aid and Sex Respect;* and Arkansas's title was *Abstinence by Choice.* Spanning several states was a *Virginity Pledge Movement,* which encourages vows from boys as well as girls.

Not surprisingly, proponents of these programs say they have been successful. They point to a decline in teenaged births, from a 1996 rate of 54.4 per 1,000 women under twenty, to 45.9 per 1,000 in 2001. Skeptics doubt that the abstinence courses are the cause. They note that the decline began in 1991, when the rate was 62.1 per 1,000, before programs like *Not Me* were installed. Nor is there direct evidence that fewer births mean teenagers were having less sex. Young people may have been just as active, but the fear of AIDS and other infections may have spurred the use of condoms. However, there are conservatives who oppose *anyone* having sex outside of marriage, even if pregnancies do not result. This helps to explain why moves to criminalize abortions have dominated the intersection of politics and sex for years.

The issue of abortion concerns what options should be open to women after they become pregnant. Most pro-life proponents believe that pregnant women should be compelled to bear their child, the rare exemptions being if her own survival is at stake, or if she is a victim of incest or rape. Their judgments that life begins at conception, and that abortions are murder, are well known. Less seldom expressed in public is their hope that if the procedure is banned, there will be less sex of the sort that now leads to clinic visits. Specifically, they feel there is too much shameless sex, before and between marriages, along with marital infidelities. Abortion gives tacit approval to this indulgence by making it easy to remedy missteps.

Underlying the opposition to abortion is the conviction that individuals and a society can become too wantonly sexualized, and that this threshold has already been reached. So they are carrying on a puritan tradition that frowns on sensual enjoyments, since they divert attention and energy from the work the world needs. For them, ideally, sex would occur only with heterosexual married partners, who love one another, and are trying their best to make a baby. The reader may estimate how many of the couplings that took place last night met all three of these conditions.

Abortion has been framed as a women's issue, if only because it is they who are the ones who get pregnant and must cope with its consequences. And the most prominent figures on the *choice* side are women, which is readily apparent by their overwhelming presence at rallies and legislative hearings. True, men who serve as lawmakers and judges often vote to uphold the right to have an abortion, just as most men generally favor its continuation. Yet what has received virtually no comment is how its being available has benefited men. We might ask what might happen if no abortions were allowed. Undoubtedly, some men would take more care with contraception. But all told, their lives would be nowhere as free—or carefree—if eggs they fertilized couldn't be excised at a clinic or a doctor's office.

Whether the conservative agenda will affect sexual decisions will be answered in the decades ahead. The most obvious indicators will be the levels of divorce, out-of-wedlock births, and the number of unmarried couples living together. But the real campaign is against ubiquitous sex. A society so overtly libidinal, from erotic soap operas to torrid advertising, impels people into bed at younger ages and with fewer formalities. Women and men are now single for longer time spans before marriage, when they are not likely to remain celibate, and the persistence of divorce augers more postmarital activity.

As has been discussed, the general view of liberals is that young people and adults are going to be sexually active, and not much can be done to stop them. So by and large they focus on advocating sex education that includes contraceptive instruction, plus the wide availability of clinics to end unplanned pregnancies. This is not to say that liberals applaud afternoon television spiced with eros and adultery. The problem is that even mild objections to such programming could sound like they're supporting censorship.

TWO SEXES, TWO NATIONS?

A decade ago, I wrote a book about race in America called *Two Nations: Black and White, Separate, Hostile, Unequal.* For a time, I considered using that title again, simply replacing *Black and White* with *Women and Men*. In the end, I decided it would be just a bit too neat. Still, its subtitle goes a long way toward describing how the sexes interact with one another—or how and where they don't.

Most people might not have a problem with using the word *unequal* when talking about the sexes. After all, there is wide agreement that women and men are still quite some distance from parity, whether gauged in social or economic terms, or attitudes inherent in the culture. We certainly know that women have less than their share of well-rewarded positions, and many feel they haven't had a fair chance, due to presumptions made by men, reinforced by their power to impose their biases.

But *unequal* carries another inference: that there are *natural* disparities between subsets of human beings. The notion that women are inferior still exists, even if not openly stated. Thus some of their supposed attributes—in particular, those associated with emotions—are cited to explain why so few women rise to head important organizations. There is also the fact that men do not take time off for pregnancy and birth; and then, for the most part, carry less of the burden of rearing children. This doesn't make men superior, but it gives them an extra edge; and once people have advantages, they often start believing they have been handed them for a reason: indeed, because they are superior.

SEXUAL HOSTILITY: MISOGYNY VS. MISANDRY

Clearly, the most somber chapter in this book was the one on rape. It sought to explain why this most depraved of assaults persists in a society that styles itself as the most advanced in the world. That chapter also took pains to say that not all men are incipient rapists. Still, the number is not infinitesimal, since rape can be defined in several ways. For example, force or intimidation needn't be used, as when a man plies a woman with alcohol, and then has his way while she is in a semiconscious condition. It was also shown that men who are usually repelled by the idea of rape can be roused by depictions of violent sex. In addition, there is the tendency to blame the victim, by making an issue out of what the woman was wearing, why she was out that late, and if she was sending signals men might construe as consent. The chapter concluded that the crime of rape arises from an abiding hatred and fear of women. Moreover, this anger drives a sufficiently large number of men to commit these offenses to a degree that is unsettling to the entire society.

The dictionary has a word for men's hatred of women: *misogyny.* While not heard every day, it occasionally crops up in literary or academic conversations. But only larger reference dictionaries list the word *misandry,* which represents an antipathy women can have for men. There are good reasons why this second word is hardly ever used, or even known. Women are certainly capable of hatred, but few of them direct their wrath against men generally. It hardly needs reiterating that many women have been used and abused by men, and some show signs of being turned off by the entire sex. In acrid tones, they depict men as self-centered, irresponsible, and worse. We can hear them telling their friends, amid knowing nods, that they are swearing off that whole half of the race. But this may not be their first such avowal, which suggests this isn't really full-blown *misandry,* since there is still the hope there could be some decent men out there. A better term is probably bitterness, which while severe, does not suggest a constitutional condition.

Men who rape dream about their next victim; and many who don't actually commit the crime have fantasies in which they subdue an unwilling partner. Yet there isn't much evidence that women have similar reveries, in which they are subduing unwilling men. In fact, we know what they *could* imagine doing: it was what one Virginia woman performed a decade ago. Well, an actual emasculation is probably too untidy to be in a fantasy. Still, masculinity can be undermined in other ways. Recall the woman researcher in the study on rape who chided men on their bicycling ability. In a similar tone after sex, women might look at their partners and ask, "Is *that* the best you can do?" Such insinuations, if widely used, could have serious effects not only on the pride but also on the potency of many men.

Yet it seems reasonable to surmise that even the bitterest of women aren't disposed to wreak that order of damage on men. Thus they do not feel a need to devise terms like *slut* and *whore* that could serve to devalue men. Part of the explanation is that they are not as frightened of men as men are of them. And if you are not possessed by fear, there is less impetus to hate, let alone to hurt and humiliate.

Where men are concerned, not many voice a generalized animus toward women. For one thing, there are not many settings nowadays where they will find companions willing to openly concur. To be sure, one may hear a man growling about some *bitch* who screwed up his life. Still, a man who whines about having been hurt by a woman doesn't look like much of a man. Also, at least at first, a generalized hatred of women seems at odds with having been in love, let alone hoping to find the girl of your dreams. But then again love—or how some men construe it—can be a seedbed for hostility. After all, it is fertile territory for anger, jealousy, possessiveness, rivalry, sensitivity to slights, pride, and so many other passions to which our species is heir to.

196

INTIMATES AND STRANGERS

Two themes intersected in the opening chapters. One was called *men's liberation,* and referred to the freedom men have to father children, and then drop out of their lives, in some cases before the baby's birth. This latitude suggests that men are freer than ever before, especially compared with the days when fathers remained with their families, due to community pressures and internal feelings of duty. If this is the case, their sex has certainly gained a lot in these shifting times. After all, it is usually women who are left to raise the children the men leave behind.

The other theme grew out of the fact that women initiate most of the nation's divorces, including those where children are involved. In addition, surveys show that more women say they wanted a marriage to end, while more of the men declared they wanted to keep it going. These findings prompt the conclusion that women have become more decisive, more willing to take a major step, and have the fortitude to face the consequences of those acts. Clearly, this is not entirely a gain for women, since after a breakup their living standard tends to decline. And having major responsibility for the children in many ways limits rather than expands their freedom. Even so, most women who have filed for a divorce will tell you that they feel freer and more in control of their lives than ever before. So we are witnessing a *women's liberation,* which grows from taking on obligations, while its male counterpart is based on abandoning them.

Which brings us to whether the sexes can be seen as *separate,* perhaps to the point of being viewed as two nations. Most people still live close to someone of the other sex, often sharing the same bed. Yet even granting this proximity, it has still been argued that men and women start off from distant planets and carry their birthmarks into adulthood. Mars and Venus may be figures of speech, but they embody important truths. Despite coeducation and living with siblings, even today most boys and girls develop distinct perceptions of themselves and their place in the world. Couples may live closely for scores of years, and yet remain strangers, barely knowing each other. They are raised as if residing in two distinct nations, which expect different outlooks and bearings from their citizen bodies.

True, there are some androgynous stirrings. Men wear pigtails and earrings, while women fill their laptops with business strategies and spreadsheets. And just as both sexes feel comfortable in jeans, so there is an affinity for entertainers who blur the boundaries associated with gender. We all know that women are entering provinces that were once the exclusive domains of men and are excelling by standards that men created. Indeed, that the sexual balance is changing has been a central theme of this book.

But even if the sexes are inching toward parity in pay and positions, on a personal level there is little evidence that the sexual divide is being bridged. Instead, there are just as many signs that the gulf is widening. It is most vividly expressed in the ubiquity of divorce. These fractures should not simply be seen as cases where a particular Jill and Jack conclude they can no longer live together. The larger reality is that half of all men and women who marry fail to make it work, and the rate is even higher for those who try again. This signals a widespread dissonance, suggesting that just because persons are of different sexes, they are not necessarily made for one another.

So the salient fact is that too few couplings flourish, to the distress of the partners and the surrounding society. Yet the hope of finding a near-perfect mate remains widespread, if not almost universal. In our pragmatic age, this is our utopian ideal: that we will somehow come across someone with whom we can ascend to celestial heights. Simply stated, the vast majority of women and men want to believe there is a Mr. Right or Ms. Right for them somewhere out there. (Along with men who are seeking their Mr. Soulmate and women searchng for their Ms. Sympatico.)

The forces propelling our times have eroded the dispositions that once enabled the sexes to live amiably together. The most notable change has been among women, whose heightened aspirations have no parallel in human times. They now spend a longer span on their own, finding out who they are and how to navigate their lives, which in turn creates a confidence they bring to their relationships. If many men say they support these outlooks and attributes, the reality is that most still hope for a measure of deference that women are no longer willing to give.

Hence an emerging mismatch between the sexes: that there are not enough men who satisfy the expectations that modern women have for dates and mates. If Sigmund Freud confessed he was never able to discern *What does a woman want?* we have some answers today. To start, women wish to be treated and regarded as full human beings, in particular by men. This standard is applied to husbands, and divorce filings reveal that more husbands than ever are failing to pass the tests their wives set. This creates another mismatch: one sex is unable to provide a pool of suitable spouses for the other. Also new in our time is a moral asymmetry, which finds increasing numbers of men and women opposed on fundamental issues. While on some occasions, opposites attract, we may wonder whether couples will stay together when one supports policies the other finds offensive.

The growing gulf is also evident in cultural interests and investments in education, in sexual orientation and commitments to parenthood. These are not developments anyone planned. The tides of history affect not only the course of nations and empires, but these forces shape each one of us. A recurring theme in this book has been that in character and constitution, we are not the manner of persons our grandparents were. If men feel less compelled to accept parental duties once assigned to their sex, women are more assured about taking over these obligations themselves. And if there are fewer submissive women, not enough men have yet shown that they are willing or able to live with a self-possessed partner.

SOURCES:

U.S. GOVERNMENT DOCUMENTS

Advance Report of Final Divorce Statistics (National Center for Health Statistics, 1995). *(FDS)*.

Advance Report of Final Marriage Statistics (National Center for Health Statistics, 1995). *(FMS)*.

America's Families and Living Arrangement (Bureau of the Census, 2001). *(AFLA)*.

Births: Final Data for 2000 (National Center for Health Statistics, 2002). *(BFD)*.

Child Support Awards for Custodial Mothers and Fathers (Bureau of the Census, 2002). *(CSA)*.

Crime in the United States (Federal Bureau of Investigation, October 2001). *(CUS)*.

Degrees and Other Awards Conferred 1999–2000 (National Center for Education Statistics, December 2001). *(DOA)*.

Detailed Characteristics 1970 (Bureau of the Census, February 1973). *(DC)*.

Digest of Education Statistics (National Center for Education Statistics, 2001). *(DES)*.

Educational Attainment in the United States (Bureau of the Census, 2000). *(EA)*.

Employment and Earnings (Bureau of Labor Statistics, 2002). *(EE)*.

Family Composition 1970 (Bureau of the Census, 1973). *(FC)*.

Fertility, Family Planning, and Women's Health (National Center for Health Statistics, 1997). *(FFP)*.

Fertility of American Women (Bureau of the Census, 2001). *(FAW)*.

First Marriage Dissolution, Divorce, and Remarriage (National Center for Health Statistics, 2001). *(FMD)*.

Living Arrangements of Children (Bureau of the Census, 2001). *(LAC)*.

Marital Status 1970 (Bureau of the Census, 1972). *(MS)*.

Money Income in the United States: March 2000 (Bureau of the Census, September 2001). *(MI)*.

SOURCES

Non-Marital Childbearing in the United States, 1940–1999 (National Center for Health Statistics, 2000). *(NMC)*.

Number, Timing, and Duration of Marriages and Divorces (Bureau of the Census, 2002). *(NTD)*.

Statistical Abstract of the United States (Bureau of the Census, 2001). *(SA)*.

Teenage Births in the United States, 1991–2000 (National Center for Health Statistics, 2002). *(TB)*.

Vital Statistics of the United States: Natality 1970 (National Center for Health Statistics, 1975). *(VSN)*.

NOTES

PREFACE

2 "wives aged 25 to 34 . . ." *Educational Attainment in the United States,* March 1998 (Bureau of the Census, October 1998).

2 "60.7 percent of divorces . . ." *FDS.*

2 "graduates of dental schools . . ." *DES.*

3 "72.9 percent of women . . . college graduates . . ." *BFD; VSN.*

3 "made more than $1 million . . ." *Statistics of Income Bulletin* (Internal Revenue Service, Winter 2001–2).

3 "non-negligent manslaughter . . ." *CUS.*

1. WHY MARRIAGES DON'T LAST

7   "husbands or wives . . ." *FC; AFLA.*

12 "they pitched in . . ." Bruce Chadwick and Tim Heaton, *Statistical Handbook on the American Family* (Oryx Press, 1999); Jane R. Wilkie et al., "Gender and Fairness: Marital Satisfaction in Two-Earner Couples, *Journal of Marriage and the Family* (August 1998).

13 "who are 35-year-old . . ." *New York Times,* October 19, 1998.

15 "the typical bride . . ." *AFLA.*

15 "their first babies . . ." *BFD; VSN.*

15 "had risen to 25.1 . . ." *AFLA.*

16 "first time for both . . ." *FMS.*

16 *"Nearly everyone marries . . ." NTD.*

16 "in their early sixties . . ." *AFLA.*

17 "entering their forties . . ." *AFLA.*

17 "ideal partners . . ." Paul Glick, *Recent Changes in American Families* (Bureau of the Census, 1975).

NOTES

2. TILL DIVORCE DO US PART

21 "lowest rate was 2.1 . . ." *FDS; Births, Marriages, Divorces, and Deaths: Provisional Data for 2001* (National Center for Health Statistics, 2002).

21 "ratio is currently about . . ." *SA.*

22 Table. *SA.*

23 "5.6 percent were divorced . . ." *AFLA; MS.*

23 "ever been divorced . . ." *Marital Characteristics 1980* (Bureau of the Census, 1985).

23 "a 52.5 percent likelihood . . ." *NTD.*

23 "marriages had children . . ." *FDS.*

24 "*rate* was 4.0 per 1,000 . . ." *Births, Marriages, Divorces, and Deaths: Provisional Data for 2001* (National Center for Health Statistics, 2002).

24 "wife was in her twenties . . ." *FDS.*

24 "one bride in six was pregnant . . ." *NMC.*

25 "lived with their husbands . . ." *FFP.*

25 "half lasted less than a year . . ." Larry Bumpass and Hsien-Hen Lu, "Trends in Cohabitation and Implications for Children's Family Contexts," *Population Studies* (March 2000).

25 "3.8 million unmarried men . . ." *AFLA.*

25 "have youngsters present . . ." *AFLA.*

26 "have reached the age of 30 . . ." *FFP.*

26 "were still intact . . ." *FFP.*

26 "outside of marriage . . ." Patricia Smock, "Cohabitation in the United States," *Annual Review of Sociology 2000* (Annual Reviews, 2001).

27 "woman is the petitioner . . ." *FDS.*

28 "women are less happy . . ." National Opinion Research Center. Unpublished printout from Tom W. Smith.

28 Table. *FDS;* Margaret Brinig and Douglas Allen, "'These Boots Are Made for Walking': Why Most Divorce Filers Are Women," *American Law and Economics Review* (Spring 2000).

29 "are physically assaulted . . ." *Intimate Partner Violence* (Bureau of Justice Statistics, May 2000).

30 "Anthony Pietropinto and Jacqueline Simenauer . . ." *Husbands and Wives: A Nationwide Survey of Marriage* (Times Books, 1979).

32 "voice-activated tape recorders . . ." Pamela Fishman, "What Do Couples Talk About When They're Alone?" in Douglas Butturff, ed. *Women's Language and Style* (University of Akron Press, 1980).

33 "sponsored by seven foundations . . ." Edward O. Laumann et al., *The Social Organization of Sexuality* (University of Chicago Press, 1994).

34 "not living with their spouse . . ." *AFLA.*

35 "married men between the ages of 40 and 44 . . ." *AFLA.*

37 "covenant marriage . . ." *New York Times,* November 10, 2001.

37 *"submit herself graciously . . ." New York Times,* June 10, 1998.

38 "another round of books . . ." James Q. Wilson, *The Marriage Problem* (HarperCollins, 2002); Barbara Dafoe Whitehood, *The Divorce Culture* (Knopf, 1997); William J. Bennett, *The Broken Hearth* (Doubleday, 2001); Maggie Gallagher, *The Abolition of Marriage* (Regnery, 1996).

39 "Nancy Dowd . . ." Nancy Dowd, *In Defense of Single-Parent Families* (New York University Press, 1999).

39 "Donna Franklin . . ." Donna Franklin, *Ensuring Inequality* (Oxford University Press, 1997).

39 *"Daddy's Roommate . . ."* Michael Willhoite, *Daddy's Roommate* (Alyson, 1991); Leslea Newman, *Heather Has Two Mommies* (Alyson, 1989).

3. DOING WITHOUT DADS

41 "in other arrangements . . ." *LAC.*

41 "30 years earlier . . ." *FC.*

42 Table. *LAC.*

43 "Stanley Lebergott . . ." Stanley Lebergott, *The American Economy: Income, Wealth, and Want* (Princeton University Press, 1976).

44 "one child in six . . ." *Speaking of Kids: A National Survey of Children and Parents* (National Commission on Children, 1991).

44 "average of 400 miles . . ." E. Mavis Hetherington and John Kelly, *For Better or for Worse* (Norton, 2002).

44 "Irwin Garfinkel . . ." *New York Times,* July 11, 1998.

45 "women are better educated . . ." *Newsweek,* May 28, 2001.

45 "more than $50,000 . . ." *MI; CSA.*

46 "16.5 percent of annual support awards . . ." *CSA.*

46 Table. *MI.*

47 Table. *CSA.*

48 "prime period for remarriage . . ." *BFD.*

48 "143 convictions . . ." *New York Times,* August 19, 2002.

49 "incomes average $12,221 . . ." *MI.*

49 "the ratio was one in twenty. . ." *SA.*

49 "In 1970, half of these children . . ." *VSN.*

50 "premarital pregancies led to marriage . . ." *NMC.*

50 Table. *SA.*

51 "Russell Sage Foundation . . ." Lawrence Wu and Barbara Wolfe (eds.), *Out-of-Wedlock: Causes and Consequences of Nonmarital Fertility* (Russell Sage, 2001).

51 "Arizona was one of four . . ." *New York Times,* September 24, 2000.

52 "teenagers are having fewer . . ." *TB.*

52 Table. *Family Planning Perspectives* (Alan Guttmacher Institute, November–December, 2001).

53 "'skills and knowledge' . . ." Wade Horn, quoted in *New York Times,* February 19, 2002.

54 "Wisconsin's supreme court . . ." *State v. Oakley* (99-3328-CR, July 10, 2001).

54 "In 2000, the Census . . ." *Poverty in the United States: 2000* (Bureau of the Census, September 2001).

55 "demanding law practice . . ." *New York Times,* July 18, 1998.

56 "how much time fathers . . ." W. Jean Yeung, "Children's Time with Fathers in Intact Families," *Journal of Marriage and the Family* (February 2001).

56 "Frank Furstenberg . . ." Quoted in *New York Times,* July 11, 1998.

56 "Paul Amato . . ." "Father-Child Relations," *Journal of Marriage and the Family* (November 1994).

56 "Francine Russo . . ." "Can the Government Prevent Divorce?" *Atlantic Monthly* (October 1997).

56 "Melissa Ludtke . . ." *On Our Own: Unmarried Motherhood in America* (Random House, 1997).

56 *"Paul Amato and Allan Booth . . ."* *A Generation at Risk* (Harvard University Press, 1997).

57 "Nicholas Wolfinger . . ." *New York Times,* August 17, 1999.

57 "single fathers accounted . . ." *FC; AFLA.*

58 "intoxicated drivers . . ." and "women were more likely . . ." *SA.*

59 "living with their fathers . . ." *AFLA.*

59 "among adults under . . ." Judith Wallerstein, *The Unexpected Legacy of Divorce* (Hyperion, 2000).

4. PASSING ON PARENTHOOD

61 "had reached their forties . . ." *FAW.*

61 "In 1970, among women . . ." *FAM.*

61 "first births to women . . ." *BFD.*

62 Table. United Nations Population Statistics Division (2002); *BFD.*

64 "'by rambunctious toddlers' . . . " Elinor Burkett, *The Baby Boon: How Family Friendly America Cheats the Childless* (Free Press, 2000).

65 "the nation's children . . ." Steve Farkas and Jean Johnson, *Kids These Days: What Americans Really Think About the Next Generation* (Public Agenda, 1997).

67 "Nathan Keyfitz . . ." "The Family That Does Not Reproduce Itself," in Kingsley Davis (ed.), *Below-Replacement Fertility in Industrial Societies* (Cambridge University Press, 1987).

68 "Kathleen Gerson . . ." *Hard Choices: How Women Decide About Work, Careers, and Motherhood* (University of California Press, 1986).

70 Table. *VSN; BFD.*
71 "Joseph Rheingold . . ." *The Fear of Being a Woman* (Grune and Stratton, 1964).
71 "Bruno Bettelheim . . ." In Jacqueline Mattfield and Carol Van Auken, eds., *Women and the Scientific Professions* (MIT Press, 1965).
73 "Department of Agriculture . . ." *Cost of Raising a Child* (Center for Nutrition Policy and Promotion, 2001).
73 "In-state students . . ." *Barron's Profiles of American Colleges 2001* (Barron's Educational Series, 2000).
75 "received returns that reported . . ." *Statistics of Income Bulletin* (Internal Revenue Service, Winter 2001–2).
76 "married couples with children . . ." *AFLA.*
78 "'wives' income' . . ." Stacy J. Rogers, "Mothers' Work Hours and Marital Quality," *Journal of Marriage and the Family* (August 1996).
78 "'spouses who become' . . ." Susan E. Crohan, "Marital Quality and Conflict Across the Transition to Parenthood," *Journal of Marriage and the Family* (November 1996).

5. EDUCATION: THE CASE OF THE MISSING MEN

80 "girls had A averages . . ." *2000 Profile of College-Bound Seniors* (College Board, 2000).
80 "to their homework . . ." *Condition of Education* (National Center for Education Statistics, 1993); *DES.*
80 "boys outnumbered girls . . ." *DES.*
81 Table. *DES.*
82 "nursery and kindergarten teachers . . ." *EE.*
84 "Higher Education Research Institute . . ." *The American Freshman Survey* (University of California at Los Angeles, 2000).
84 Table. *Profile of College-Bound Seniors* (College Board, 2000).
86 Table. *American Colleges and Universities* (American Council on Education, 1970); *Barron's Profiles of American Colleges* (Barron's Educational Series, 2001).
88 Table. *Profile of College-Bound Seniors* (College Board, 2000).
91 "only 38.9 percent of the girls . . ." Ann M. Gallagher, *Sex Differences in the Performance of High-Scoring Examinees on the SAT-M* (College Board, 1990).
92 "girls who might have done better . . ." Ann M. Gallagher, *Sex Differences in Problem-Solving Strategies Used by High-Scoring Examinees on the SAT-M* (College Board, 1992).
93 Table. The College Board.

6. THE DOUBLE STANDARD:
HOW MUCH HAS REALLY CHANGED?

 99 "one bride in ten . . ." *NMC.*
100 "haven't yet married . . ." *AFLA.*
101 "average of 3.5 different . . ." Edward O. Laumann et al., *The Social Organization of Sexuality* (University of Chicago Press, 1994).
102 Table. *FFP.*
104 Table. *AFLA.*
105 "who had been married . . ." *AFLA.*
106 Table. *FMS.*
107 "'if women's liberation' . . ." Gloria Steinem, "What It Would Be Like If Women Win," *Time,* August 31, 1970.

7. THE FRAGILITY OF MASCULINITY

109 "garage mechanics . . ." *EE.*
111 "637,511 law enforcement officers . . ." *SA.*
112 "66 executions . . ." *SA.*
113 Table. *Washington Post* polls, August 2000 to January 2001.
116 "sales of Viagra . . ." Pfizer advertisement, *New York Times,* May 6, 2001.
116 "three quarters of the men . . ." Edward O. Laumann et al., *The Social Organization of Sexuality* (University of Chicago Press, 1994).
117 "54 percent of women voters . . ." *New York Times,* November 12, 2000.
118 "a million black men . . ." *Prisoners in 2001* (Bureau of Justice Statistics, 2002).
119 "Title IX of the Education Act . . ." *New York Times,* May 9, 2002.
119 "women's teams rose . . ." *Chronicle of Higher Education,* May 18, 2001.
120 Table. New York Roadrunners Club. Unpublished figures.
121 "Stanford's women's volleyball team . . ." "The Big College Try," *New York Review of Books,* April 12, 2001.
121 "fewer women than men were overweight . . ." *SA.*
121 "'regular vigorous activity' . . ." *Physical Activity and Health* (National Center for Chronic Disease Prevention, 1999).

8. THE ULTIMATE ASSAULT:
WHY RAPE PERSISTS

124 "90,186 reports of rape . . ." *CUS.*

124 "victimization survey . . ." *Criminal Victimization 2000* (Bureau of Justice Statistics, 2001).

125 "face-to-face interviews . . ." *Prevalence, Incidences, and Consequences of Violence Against Women* (National Institute of Justice, 1998).

125 "Massachusetts high school . . ." *Journal of the American Medical Association* (August 1, 2001).

125 "3,187 college women . . ." *Sexual Victimization of College Women* (Bureau of Justice Statistics, 2000).

125 "a sample of college men . . ." Michael Ghiglieri, *The Dark Side of Man* (Perseus, 1999).

126 Table. Lawrence A. Greenfield, *Sex Offenses and Offenders* (Bureau of Justice Statistics, 1997).

127 "Howard Barbaree . . ." *Journal of Clinical and Consulting Psychology* (October 1991).

128 "Susan Brownmiller . . ." *Against Our Will* (Simon & Schuster, 1975).

129 "Michael Ghiglieri . . ." *The Dark Side of Man* (Perseus, 1999).

133 "'need to examine' . . ." Robert Prentky et al., "Validation Analyses on a Taxonomic System for Rapists," *Annals of the New York Academy of Sciences* (January 1988).

9. HOMOSEXUALITY:
AN EMERGING ALTERNATIVE

139 "Dorothy Dinnerstein . . ." *The Mermaid and the Minotaur* (Harper and Row, 1976).

139 "Betty Jean Lifton . . ." *Journey of the Adopted Self* (Basic Books, 1994).

139 "The Census estimated . . ." *LAC.*

140 "*Journal of Abnormal Psychology* . . ." Henry Adams et al., "Is Homophobia Associated with Homosexual Arousal?" (August 1994).

141 "more than two to one . . ." Bruce Chadwick and Tim Heaton, *Statistical Handbook on the American Family* (Oryx, 1999).

142 "1.4 percent of the women . . ." Edward O. Laumann et al., *The Social Organization of Sexuality* (University of Chicago Press, 1994).

143 "'gay until graduation' . . ." *New York Times,* July 2, 1997.

146 Table. *AFLA; MS.*

10. THE BLACK EXPERIENCE:
A PORTENT FOR WHITES

149 "His analysis was brutal . . ." Daniel Patrick Moynihan, *The Negro Family: The Case for National Action* (Department of Labor, 1965).

150 Table. *MI;* Census P-60 Series, 1950 through 1990.

152 "white men aged 35 to 44 . . ." *MI.*

154 "were first published . . ." *DES.*

154 "70 percent of rap recordings . . ." Stephen Slaybaugh, "Into the Mainstream," *Columbus Alive Wired* (July 13–19, 2000).

154 "85 percent of the seats . . ." David Shields, *Black Planet: Facing Race During an NBA Season* (Three Rivers Press, 1999), plus communication from the author.

156 Table. *BFD; VSN.*

157 "are virtually identical . . ." *BFD.*

157 "pregnant single women . . ." *FFP.*

159 Table. *AFLA; MS.*

160 Table. *DOA; EE; DC.*

161 "Interracial marriages . . ." *AFLA.*

11. PAY, POSITIONS, POWER:
INCHING TOWARD EQUITY

163 "men rank well ahead . . ." *MI.*

165 Table. *MI;* plus Census P-60 series, 1950–1990.

166 "Marvin Harris . . ." *America Now: The Anthropology of a Changing Culture* (Simon & Schuster, 1982).

168 Table. *EE; DC.*

170 "all retiring men . . ." *Annual Statistical Supplement to the Social Security Bulletin: 1999* (Social Security Administration, 2000).

170 "those between the ages of 60 and 64 . . ." *MI; DC.*

171 Table. *Employee Tenure in 2000* (Bureau of Labor Statistics, 2000).

172 Table. *MI; EA.*

173 *"Fortune . . ." Fortune,* April 15, 2002.

175 "America's 400 wealthiest individuals . . ." *Forbes,* October 8, 2001.

177 "women's basketball teams . . ." "The Big College Try," *New York Review of Books* (April 12, 2001).

177 "Morgan Stanley . . ." Advertisement in *New York Times,* January 7, 2002.

177 "250 leading firms . . ." *National Law Journal,*" September 30, 2001.

179 "husbands are retired . . ." *New York Times,* June 24, 2001.

180 "Sylvia Ann Hewlett . . ." *A Lesser Life: The Myth of Women's Liberation in America* (Morrow, 1986).

180 "Catalyst . . ." *Women in Financial Services,* July 25, 2001.

181 Table. *MI.*

12. THE PAIRING PROBLEM

186 "among unmarried voters . . ." *New York Times,* November 12, 2000.

187 "two sets of individuals . . ." *MI.*

189 "1,514 girls and 963 boys . . ." "Looking Backward," in Peter Salins, ed., *New York Unbound* (Blackwell, 1988).

189 "levels of the nation's married couples . . ." *Educational Attainment in the United States 1998* (Bureau of the Census, 1998).

191 "Speaker of the House . . ." J. Dennis Hastert, *New York Times,* April 11, 2002.

192 "fifteen-year-old girls . . ." *FFP.*

192 *"Not Me, Not Now . . ."* Sharon Lerner, "Bush's Marriage Proposal," *Village Voice,* May 1, 2002.

192 "decline in teenaged . . ." *TB.*

194 "a book about race . . ." Andrew Hacker, *Two Nations: Black and White, Separate, Hostile, Unequal* (Scribner, 1992).

ACKNOWLEDGMENTS

Mismatch has profited immensely from the care and attention of four editors. Gillian Blake and Nan Graham at Scribner offered every kind of encouragement an author wants and needs. Bill Goldstein and Mindy Werner went over each line and improved every one of them. This is the third book of mine that Erich Hobbing has designed, and I look forward to many more. Rachel Sussman was particularly helpful in the book's final stages. And the keen eye of copy editor Estelle Laurence caught what could have been some embarrassing errors.

Robin Straus, my agent and friend for many years, has always been on hand with counsel and understanding, not only for my books but throughout my professional career. Claudia Dreifus, to whom *Mismatch* is dedicated, provided both affection and inspiration, along with the subtle support that one writer knows how to give to another.

Parts of this book first appeared, in somewhat different forms, in review-essays for *The New York Review of Books*. I am grateful to that publication for permission to reprint this material. And I owe particular thanks to Robert Silvers and Barbara Epstein for their continuing encouragement and incisive suggestions.

When people asked what I was working on, and they heard the subject, many helpful conversations ensued. So my thanks to these friends and acquaintances, as well as to professional colleagues who assisted me with information and ideas: Peter Brimelow, Andrew Cherlin, Alyson Cole, Robert Cornish, Mary Cox, Betsy Dexheimer, Beatrice Dreifus, Kathy Eden, Benita Eisler, Edward Jay Epstein, Jim

ACKNOWLEDGMENTS

and Sondra Farganis, William and Joan Friedland, Rosemary Fogerty, Ester Fuchs, Frank Furstenberg, Janice Gams, John Gerassi, Kathleen Gerson, Carol Gilligan, Ann and Tim Gower, Helen Hacker, Jere Herzenberg, Michael Iovenko, Jerry Jacobs, Oren Jarinkes, Harvey Jay, Joseph Kanon, Ann Kjellberg, Ethel Klein, Chuck Kleinhans, Lilian Kohlreiser, Edward Laumann, Amy Lawrence, Susanne Leisy, Julia Lesage, Kristin Luker, Alison Lurie, Nancy Macomber, Douglas Massey, Nancy Newhouse, Wentworth Ofuatey-Kodjoe, Patricia Rachal, Sam Roberts, Joe Rollins, Barbara Sand, Richard Sandomir, Jennifer Schuessler, Allen Sessoms, David Shields, Christina Hoff Sommers, Monica Strauss, Deborah Tannen, Sandra Thornton, Joan Tronto, Stephanie Ventura, Roger Wilkins, and Garry Wills.

INDEX

INDEX

Magerko, Maggie, 176
Mailer, Norman, 153
Maine, 22
Malta, 61
Managers and executives
  women, 173–81
    percentage of blacks who are, 159, 160
    whether they had children, 180–81
  See also Income—by sex
Manheim, Camryn, 45
Marathon, New York City, 120, 121
Marriageable men, 186–87
Marriages, 7–20
  abusive, 29–30
  adultery in, 33–36, 38, 193, 194
  for better or for worse, 11
  childlessness in, 59, 65–67
  complementarity in, 3–5, 18–19, 78, 137
  conflict in, and children, 56–57
  couples living apart in, 34
  covenant, 37, 191
  failure rate of, 7–8
  fewer children in, 50, 61
  ideal partners in, 17–20, 198
  interracial, 119, 161
  living together as alternative to, 7
  multiple, 16–17
  non-marital children in, 50–51
  number of people in, 7, 16–17, 138, 145–46
    black vs. white women, 160–61
  politics of, 37–39, 185–86
  postponing of, 69–71
  pregnancy as reason for, 15, 24, 50, 99
  premarital education for, 191–92
  of professional, high-income women, 105, 106
  purpose of, 8
  reasons for, 9–11
  searching for partners for, 14–16, 185–99
  "shortage" of men for, 147, 158, 161
  why some last, 17–20
  women's and men's attitudes to, 11–14
  See also Divorces; Husbands; Unmarried couples; Wives
Martinique, 61, 63
Marty (movie), 190–91
Maryland, 22
Masculinity, 109–22
  and attitude toward gays, 140, 141
  culture of, 110–13, 176–79
  nature of, 114–15
  race and, 117–19
  woman's judging of, 115–16
  See also Fathers; Husbands; Men
Masochistic sex, 131
Massachusetts, 22
Maternal instinct, 71
Mates, searching for, 14–16, 185–99
Mathematics, 80, 91–95
Mauritius, 61
Maxim (magazine), 13
MBAs, 81, 159, 175, 177
Medicine
  graduates in (MDs), 81, 159, 167, 168
  key to success in, 178
Men
  accusatory terms against, 98–99
  ambiguity rejected by, 144
  fantasies of, 115, 127, 135
  ideological doctrines of, 72
  intelligence of, 79
  marriageable, 186–87
  misogynic, 195–96
  never married, 16–17, 145–46
  number of sexual partners of, 101–2